Artificial Intelligence Fundamentals: Understanding Modern Machine Learning Concepts

Discover AI Basics Through Approachable, Real-World Examples

Theodore Vale

Table of Contents

INTRODUCTION

Artificial intelligence is not a far-off concept limited to science fiction; rather, it is already here and entwined into our daily lives. Artificial intelligence is changing our means of living, employment, and interaction with the environment. This covers all from facial recognition and autonomous cars to voice assistants and smart recommendations. Still, many people find great difficulty understanding the workings of these intelligent systems.

"Artificial Intelligence Fundamentals: Understanding Modern Machine Learning Concepts - Discover AI Basics Through Approachable, Real-World Examples" is conveniently available and your first point of contact into the amazing realm of artificial intelligence and machine learning. To follow along, you only need an inquisitive mind and a wish to understand the way in which the technology influencing our future actually runs; you do not need to be a computer scientist or mathematician. Every chapter explores the basic concepts, investigates useful algorithms, and offers instances of how artificial intelligence is applied in daily life, including image recognition and language translation, as well as examples of how artificial intelligence is used in business.

By means of this program, you will not only acquire basic knowledge but also gain insights into the ethical concerns and social impact related to artificial intelligence. Whether you are getting ready for a future completely furnished with technology or just want to know the buzz about artificial intelligence, this book will give you the clarity and self-assurance you need to participate in the conversation.

CHAPTER I

What is Artificial Intelligence?

Defining AI in the Modern World - Explore how AI is perceived today, from simple automation to advanced cognitive systems

One of the most revolutionary technologies to surface in the modern era is artificial intelligence, sometimes known as AI. The boundaries of what machines are able to accomplish are changing, as is the way they can support, improve, and even challenge human capacities. The definition of artificial intelligence in the modern world encompasses much more than just the straightforward idea of robots or computers completing tasks. Artificial intelligence includes robots and computers. It covers a large terrain of artificial intelligence systems capable of learning, adapting, reasoning, and responding to data and stimuli in ways that are either similar to or complementary to human intelligence. These systems can reason, grow, adapt, and learn. Artificial intelligence (AI) is not a concept reserved for science fiction in the future in the modern world; rather, it is a real, tangible part of daily life ingrained in everything from virtual assistants and smartphone apps to major industrial automation and scientific research.

The most basic definition of artificial intelligence is the ability of computers and mechanical tools to replicate some features of human intelligence. One finds this definition in the field of computer science. Learning from experience, identifying trends, understanding language, solving problems, and making decisions are a few of the activities that fall under this category. Building systems that can carry out cognitive tasks usually connected with the human mind will help us to reach the aims of this project. On the other hand, the definition of artificial intelligence applied nowadays is more complex than those used in the past. Early definitions of artificial intelligence concentrated on the creation of machines able to execute any intellectual activity a human being could. Modern artificial intelligence is often goal-oriented, meaning it is meant to solve particular problems by using data, algorithms, and computational capability. Many artificial intelligence systems are meant to perform specific tasks with an efficiency higher than human ability, not to replicate the whole spectrum of human intelligence.

Among the most important features of modern artificial intelligence technologies is their dependence on data. Artificial intelligence (AI) systems differ from conventional computer programs, which follow rigid, rule-based instructions in that AI systems learn from data to guide decisions. Machine learning is the process by which systems identify trends, generate predictions, and, over time, raise their performance. This process also goes under the names deep learning and reinforcement learning. Supervised learning is the kind of learning in which training algorithms learn the link between inputs and outputs by means of labelled datasets. Among the several kinds of learning, this one is one. Unsupervised learning is the study of data without reference to predefined labels with an aim to expose latent structures or groupings. Finding latent features is the aim of this procedure. By means of trial and error, reinforcement learning enables artificial intelligence agents to acquire ideal behaviours. This helps the agents to pick the most sensible behaviour. This feedback can take the form of corrections or rewards. These learning paradigms form the basis of contemporary artificial intelligence systems since they enable these systems to execute challenging tasks, including image recognition, speech processing, and strategic game playing.

Artificial intelligence (AI) shows itself in a range of less obvious forms in today's environment, yet it is also firmly embedded in daily life. It is getting harder to tell these approaches apart from one another. Natural language processing and speech recognition let virtual assistants like Siri, Alexa, and Google Assistant understand and answer user questions. The fact that these assistants can answer user questions and grasp helps to enable this capacity. These systems help to interpret meaning, create responses appropriate for the circumstances, and even perform chores, including reminders or music playing. To complete these chores, they depend on large databases and sophisticated algorithms. Likewise, recommendation systems on websites including Netflix, Amazon, and Spotify examine user behaviour to provide content that fits personal tastes. This is undertaken to give consumers the best possible streaming experience. Conversely, these systems constitute instances of limited artificial intelligence. Though they lack general intelligence or understanding, these systems are programs meant to be quite good at performing particular tasks.

In many other sectors, including healthcare, finance, transportation, and manufacturing, the use of artificial intelligence has also brought about transforming changes. Artificial intelligence-powered tools are being used in the field of medicine to help with the diagnosis of diseases, image analysis, patient outcome prediction, and even the creation of individualized treatment plans. Algorithms trained on vast databases of clinical images and medical records can identify patterns that might be challenging even for the most seasoned experts. Difficult to identify patterns can be found in these algorithms. In the financial industry, artificial intelligence is being applied for a range of uses, including creditworthiness determination, trading automation, fraud detection, and strategic optimization of investments. By means of artificial intelligence (AI), autonomous cars can understand sensor data, identify objects, and make decisions about real-time driving based on This brings us one step toward a time when transportation can run free from human control. Driven by artificial intelligence, robotics and predictive maintenance systems help to raise manufacturing industry product quality.

Artificial intelligence (AI) remains difficult to define even if it is becoming more and more popular and has a growing capacity. This is so because it covers a rather broad spectrum of technologies and techniques. Technological developments mean that what we now define as artificial intelligence (AI) might not be such in the future. Artificial intelligence (AI) was first celebrated in the 1950s and 1960s as basic rule-based programs that solved arithmetic problems or engaged in chess. These initiatives successfully addressed issues. For several reasons, these same programs are regarded as quite primitive in today's world when compared to deep learning models, which can create realistic images from scratch or produce text that is shockingly similar to that of humans. Referred to as the "AI effect," this phenomenon reflects a changing view whereby artificial intelligence systems—once they start to become conventional or well understood—are no longer regarded as really intelligent. This change of view reflects the coining of the term "AI effect."

Often mentioned in the framework of the modern era are three different forms of artificial intelligence: narrow artificial intelligence, general artificial intelligence, and superintelligent artificial intelligence. Narrow artificial intelligence, sometimes known as weak artificial intelligence, is the term used to characterize systems intended to perform particular tasks within particular environments. These are, thus, right now, the most common and useful applications of artificial intelligence. Though they might have extraordinary abilities in a given field, such as language translation or facial recognition, it is not possible for them to extend their knowledge to other sectors. Within the framework of artificial intelligence, strong artificial intelligence—also known as general artificial intelligence—is the hypothetical capacity of a system to execute any intellectual task that a human being is qualified for. This degree of artificial intelligence would depend on one being able to reason, learn, and plan. It also would be imperative for it to be able to understand abstract ideas, context, and emotions. Though overall artificial intelligence is still a long-term goal for study, it has not yet been reached. Intelligent systems that are better than human intelligence in practically all spheres, including creativity, problem-solving, and social intelligence, are referred to as "superintelligent artificial intelligence" (AI). We refer to these systems as artificial intelligence systems. Though its future is yet unknown, this idea is now under discussion both ethically and theoretically in the field of philosophy.

Defining artificial intelligence (AI) in the modern world calls for careful thought given ethical issues. As artificial intelligence keeps becoming more powerful and ubiquitous, questions about its fairness, transparency, responsibility, and impact on society abound. Given that artificial intelligence is expected to keep developing, these issues are founded in For instance, the presence of bias in artificial intelligence systems might result in unfair results in many spheres, including law enforcement, lending, and recruiting candidates. Should the data used to train an artificial intelligence model reflect historical prejudices or inequalities, it is conceivable that the model will either reinforce or even magnify these biases. This is so because the training data used reflects past prejudices of the model. Apart from their varied presence in the teams in charge of creating artificial intelligence, these kinds of issues call for meticulous design, testing, and control. Important phases are designing, testing, and controlling. Furthermore, the lack of openness causes great worry. Many artificial intelligence systems—especially those based on deep learning—function as "black boxes"; that is, they make decisions without offering obvious justification. In the field of deep learning especially, this is particularly true. In high-stakes fields like criminal justice or healthcare, where understanding the reasoning behind decisions is crucial, this lack of interpretability can be troublesome.

Another important factor defining artificial intelligence in the modern era is the link it has with the workforce. Given artificial intelligence's ability to learn to automate more chores, questions about job displacement and economic inequality have grown in frequency. For example, routine, repetitious jobs are especially prone to be automated. Conversely, fresh prospects could arise in domains connected to the evolution of artificial intelligence, data science, and human-AI cooperation. Preparing workers for this change will mostly depend on retraining and education, which will guarantee that the advantages of artificial intelligence are shared among many people. Artificial intelligence will help to bring about this change. Many experts see a future in which artificial intelligence will augment human capabilities, allowing people to focus on creative problem-solving, empathy, and complex problem-solving rather than totally replace them. To help one understand this, consider the situation whereby artificial intelligence would totally replace humans.

Apart from its ramifications in the pragmatic and financial domains, artificial intelligence (AI) raises philosophical and existential concerns about the nature of intelligence and consciousness. To what degree, then, can a machine experience emotions or understand them? If an artificial entity possessed self-awareness or a sense of morality, would it be possible for it to be artificial? These questions are the reason our perspective of what it means to be intelligent or even human is under doubt. Constant advancements in cognitive modelling and brain-computer interfaces challenge human-machine interaction limits. Constant research and development help to produce these developments. Though the systems now in use lack consciousness or subjective experience, these developments kept stretching the boundaries of what is feasible with artificial intelligence.

The ability of artificial intelligence to be coupled with other technologies is another feature that distinguishes it from other developing technologies in modern society. To create intelligent and linked systems, artificial intelligence (AI) is progressively being mixed with other disciplines including the Internet of Things (IoT), robotics, augmented reality (AR), virtual reality (VR), and blockchain. One is doing this in order to create artificial intelligence. Smart homes can automatically run daily activities and recognize the preferences of their occupants by means of artificial intelligence. Artificial intelligence is essential for industrial Internet of Things systems serving predictive maintenance and quality control. Artificial intelligence-powered augmented reality and virtual reality experiences create interactive and immersive settings for the entertainment sector. The combination of these technologies creates artificial intelligence potential, which in turn enables the development of more dynamic, flexible, customized solutions spanning many sectors.

The worldwide competition for artificial intelligence leadership offers still another evidence of the strategic relevance of artificial intelligence in geopolitics. Countries all around the world are making major expenditures in artificial intelligence research and development as well as infrastructure. These expenditures are being made with the goal of acquiring a competitive advantage in the domains of defence, economic output, and technical innovation. Among the nations trying to create national artificial intelligence (AI) strategies are the United States of America, China, and members of the European Union. These approaches are meant to inspire creativity, solve moral issues, and guarantee responsible application of artificial intelligence. Artificial intelligence is not only a technical development; rather, it is a major determinant of national security and worldwide impact. This global momentum has resulted in the general understanding of the reality that artificial intelligence is not only a technical development.

Regarding the field of education, the way artificial intelligence shapes our instruction and learning process also fits the definition of artificial intelligence in contemporary language. Platforms driven by artificial intelligence naturally enable the personalizing of learning experiences, content adaptation to the particular needs of every individual, and real-time feedback provision. Intelligent tutoring systems help students struggling with demanding courses since they can pinpoint areas of weakness and modify their instruction. These systems can certainly help to accomplish this. Concurrent with this is the obligation of educational institutions and teachers to take ethical issues of data privacy, algorithmic bias, and the need for human supervision in digital education technologies under consideration.

Another necessary component of the modern definition of artificial intelligence is the general understanding of computer programs by the people. Though artificial intelligence permeates every facet of life, many people still have limited or erroneous ideas of what kind of things it can and cannot do. The way artificial intelligence is portrayed in popular culture often results in an overstatement of its powers, which then fuels inappropriate expectations and worries. Closing this knowledge gap by means of easily available education, public discourse, and open communication is indispensable for the growth of trust and the encouragement of responsible innovation. One can achieve this with easily available education. In the framework of debates about artificial intelligence policy and control, as well as the consequences it will have on society, people have an obligation to engage in those conversations with a high degree of knowledge.

Given the continuous evolution of artificial intelligence (AI), it is quite likely that the definition of AI will grow and change to fit fresh ideas and applications. The basic idea, however, has not changed: the use of machines to copy or improve features of human intelligence in ways that are useful, effective, and significant. This is the idea that has stayed constant. In the framework of the modern world, artificial intelligence (AI) is not a single entity; rather, it is a varied and always changing collection of tools, techniques, and philosophies reflecting our goals, values, and challenges throughout the course of human history. It not only shows the kind of future we wish to build for ourselves using technology but also reflects our capacity for achievement with regard to this.

Defining artificial intelligence in the modern world goes beyond just summarizing its technical features or enumeration of uses. This is so because defining artificial intelligence calls for many distinct components. One must thus have a thorough awareness of the ethical aspects of artificial intelligence, its interaction with other technologies, its part in society, and its ability to shape the future of mankind. One must acquire this understanding. The demand for considerate, inclusive, and well-informed conversation is rising steadily as artificial intelligence (AI) finds more and more applications in our daily lives. By means of real-world examples and ideas anchored in reality, the study of artificial intelligence helps us transcend the hype and concern surrounding it. This will help us to adopt a viewpoint on this amazing field that is both more subtle and more empowering. Whether we are consumers, creators, or users, every one of us has a stake in the narrative of artificial intelligence and can help to write the next chapter in its course.

A Brief History of AI Development - Discuss the evolution of AI, from early rule-based systems to modern deep learning

People have always been inquisitive, driven, and unrelenting in their quest of the aim of producing machines capable of thinking, learning, and solving problems. Artificial intelligence's history is this. Artificial intelligence has evolved over seven decades of scientific advancement and thousands of years of imagination, spanning both ancient stories that started it and modern neural networks that finished it. The interaction of technical innovation, philosophical investigation, and social change has shaped the field of artificial intelligence into what it is now. Knowing this path not only clarifies the interaction of three elements but also helps to contextualize the developments in artificial intelligence nowadays. Artificial intelligence has developed in cycles of excitement, progress, setbacks, and resurgence instead of a straight-line evolution. Usually referred to as the boom-and-bust periods of artificial intelligence, these cycles Regarding trying to replicate facets of human intelligence in machines, these cycles mirror both the great potential and the great difficulties involved in the project.

Artificial intelligence has its roots in prehistoric societies where the idea was first developed. Greek mythology had legends of clever automaton creation. One instance of this is the massive bronze man Hephaestus built to protect the island of Crete. Aristotle and other thinkers set the stage for logical thinking, which would subsequently form the foundation for formal logic systems applied in artificial intelligence. The idea of artificial life that could think or act at the human level has captivated people's imaginations for millennia. Conversely, modern computing emerged only in the 20th century, so separating these ideas from the domain of myth and philosophy and into the field of science and engineering.

Often cited as the occasion that formally launched artificial intelligence as a field of research is the Dartmouth Conference, held in the summer of 1956. Considered especially important were the eminent researchers John McCarthy, Marvin Minsky, Nathaniel Rochester, and Claude Shannon, who attended this event. The scholars argued that "every aspect of learning or any other feature of intelligence can in principle be so precisely described that a machine can be made to simulate it." This audacious declaration established the term "artificial intelligence" itself and shaped future AI research direction. It also coined the term "artificial intelligence." Early studies on artificial intelligence in the late 1950s and early 1960s focused mostly on symbolic thinking and problem-solving. Frequently referred to as "good old-fashioned artificial intelligence," these systems depended on explicit rules and logic to perform their tasks. Programs like the Logic Theorist, created by Allen Newell and Herbert A. Simon, were among the first to show that machines could solve mathematical problems in ways that resembled human reasoning.

There was a lot of hope during the 1960s. Researchers thought that given enough rules and computational capability, machines could attain human-level intelligence even in a matter of decades. Advancements in the translation of languages, the evolution of systems for the playing of games, and fundamental reasoning occurred during this time span. Developed by Joseph Weizenbaum and intended to replicate the behaviour of a Rogerian psychotherapist, one prominent example is the early natural language processing program ELIZA. ELIZA was able to enthral users and show the promise of conversational agents even though her responses consisted of basic pattern matches instead of real comprehension. Conversely, early artificial intelligence systems soon showed their flaws. These programs were unable to handle ambiguity or the complexity of the real world; their sole ability to solve highly specific problems was Their knowledge could not be acquired by experience or generalized outside of the guidelines they had been taught to follow.

Often referred to as the "AI winter," a notable slowing down in the evolution of artificial intelligence started in the 1970s as the first excitement gave way to disappointment and reduced funding and interest in artificial intelligence research. Government agencies and private sponsors who had earlier supported AI projects began pulling their money since their expectations were not satisfied and the advancement made was slow. Expert systems were brittle and challenging to scale; first, machine translating systems yielded poor results, and speech recognition was limited to a small number of predefined words. Critics claimed that artificial intelligence (AI) had overstated promises and that its useful applications remained elusive. During this period, researchers were obliged to rethink their approaches, which produced a phase of artificial intelligence research more grounded and cautious.

Originally developed in the late 1970s and early 1980s, expert systems helped to briefly revive artificial intelligence (AI) interest despite subsequent disappointments. Designed to replicate the decision-making capacity of human experts in one or more particular domains, expert systems depended on a knowledge base with facts and rules in addition to an inference engine applying those rules for the aim of solving problems. One well-known instance is the MYCIN system, created at Stanford University to identify bacterial infections and provide antibiotic recommendations. Expert systems have been adopted by several sectors, including engineering, finance, and medicine; some of these systems have even attained commercial success. They needed continuous updates from human experts since they found it challenging to finish tasks outside of their scope. They also presented costly building and maintenance expenses. Expert systems' shortcomings became clear over time, which led to still another dampening of interest in artificial intelligence.

In the late 1980s and early 1990s, machine learning became a respectable method for artificial intelligence, so transforming the discipline of artificial intelligence. Unlike rule-based systems from the past, machine learning lets computers learn patterns from data without explicit programming for every conceivable scenario. Development in statistical techniques, algorithmic approaches, and computational capability all working together helped to enable this change in paradigm. This change was much influenced by the comeback of neural networks, which derived from the structure and purpose of the human brain. Early iterations of neural networks struggled to solve challenging problems because of constraints in training algorithms and computing resources. This was even though several decades earlier, many had conceptualized neural networks. Backpropagation is a useful technique for training multi-layer neural networks that helped to revive interest in connectionist models and create the foundation for the next developments.

Additionally notable developments in artificial intelligence that caught the public's interest during the 1990s decade were In a 1997 match that will go down in history, IBM's Deep Blue beat reigning world chess champion Garry Kasparov. This triumph proved that, in highly regimented fields with clear rules, machines can outperform humans. Deep Blue was a major accomplishment in the field of artificial intelligence capabilities, but its success was not due to general intelligence but rather to brute-force computation and strategic evaluation. Researchers began investigating machine learning approaches, including support vector machines, decision trees, and other approaches that showed to be successful for jobs including pattern recognition, classification, and regression about the same time.

The decade of the 2000s marked the start of a new era in the evolution of artificial intelligence as a result of the exponential increase of data, developments in computing power, and the expansion of the Internet. While hardware was developing, especially graphics processing units (GPUs), which enabled more quick and efficient computation, the explosion of big data made it feasible to train machine learning models using enormous volumes of data at the same time. Applications using machine learning first began to be rather extensively used during this era. From spam filters, search engines, recommendation systems, and fraud detection algorithms, the degree of sophistication and dependability of each kept growing. These practical uses proved the value of artificial intelligence over a broad range of corporate sectors and helped the public to trust it.

Deep learning, a subfield of machine learning using vast-scale neural networks with many layers (hence the term "deep"), was the true breakthrough in the 2010s. Particularly convolutional neural networks (CNNs) and recurrent neural networks (RNNs), deep learning models performed state-of-the-art in a range of applications, including image recognition, speech synthesis, language translation, and game playing. Developed by University of Toronto researchers, a deep learning model won the ImageNet contest by a notable margin in 2012, much above conventional computer vision methods. Among the most famous events in the annals of computer vision is thought to be this one. This occasion marked the start of the revolution in deep learning and acted as the impetus for a spike of artificial intelligence (AI) interest, investment, and creativity.

DeepMind's deep reinforcement learning system AlphaGo was able to outplay Lee Sedol, the current world champion in the game of Go, which is far more challenging than chess. 2016 saw another historic event as well. AlphaGo's success surprised the general people as well as the artificial intelligence community. Go had been considered for a long time as a challenge beyond the reach of machines because of its vast search area and the importance of intuition. AlphaGo used deep learning in concert with Monte Carlo tree search and self-play reinforcement learning to show a fresh degree of artificial intelligence sophistication and adaptability. This achievement not only proved that artificial intelligence can master challenging tasks but also motivated more study on naturally generalizable learning systems.

Large-scale language models brought about a comparable leap forward in the field of natural language processing (NLP). Early systems such as Word2Vec and

GloVe helped to improve word representation in vector space, so enabling a more complex knowledge of the language. Transformer architectures—more especially, Google's BERT and OpenAI's GPT series—revolutionized natural language processing (N LP). These designs enabled models to more successfully capture relationships and context inside text. These models attained a degree of performance never seen before in jobs, including sentiment analysis, text generation, machine translation, and question answering. Having 175 billion parameters, GPT-3 proved capable of producing coherent, human-like text over a broad spectrum of subjects. This spurred debates on authorship, the creative possibilities of artificial intelligence, and the limits separating human from machine expression.

As artificial intelligence (AI) has expanded capabilities, ethical, biassed, privacy, and more general societal consequences of intelligent systems have grown more of a concern. Artificial intelligence raises serious issues about the suitable governance of these technologies since it has the capacity to aggravate already existing inequalities, change public opinion, or automate surveillance. Researchers, legislators, business leaders, and others have started to advocate for values in artificial intelligence design and deployment, including openness, responsibility, justice, and inclusivity. Aimed at addressing these issues and guaranteeing that artificial intelligence serves the public good, such projects including explainable artificial intelligence (XAI), responsible artificial intelligence frameworks, and multidisciplinary collaborations were Therefore, the history of artificial intelligence consists not only in the technical achievements but also in the growing awareness of the human values and society structures moulded by technology and hence shaped by it.

Over the 2020s, this pattern of fast development and introspection has continued. Artificial intelligence systems are now starting to be included in critical infrastructure, healthcare, education, transportation, and communication. The development of multimodal models, including data from text, images, audio, and video, has extended the spectrum of applications for artificial intelligence even more. Generative artificial intelligence models, including ChatGPT, DALL-E, and others, have proven able to create text, images, music, and even software code. This has spurred major questions about authenticity, innovation, and the very core of intelligence itself. Simultaneously, scientists are trying to scale artificial intelligence models in a more effective way, lower their energy usage, and increase their accessibility to a larger spectrum of users and developers.

The evolution of artificial intelligence over its whole history has been distinguished by a dynamic interaction between imagination and implementation, hope and caution, discovery and discipline. From its beginnings in mythology to its integration into modern society, artificial intelligence has been a mirror of mankind's relentless search to understand and replicate its own intelligence in all phases of its evolution. Computer science, mathematics, neuroscience, psychology, linguistics, philosophy, and ethics have all helped to shape this field—which has grown ever more complicated over time. Artificial intelligence (AI) is developing, and its past not only records achievements but also provides a point of reference for negotiating the challenging terrain ahead. Artificial intelligence's path is not nearly complete, and every new discovery adds still another layer to this already complex and always growing narrative. Knowing where artificial intelligence (AI) has come from helps one to understand where it might be headed in the future and how we, as a society, might responsibly and sensibly shape its future.

Everyday Applications of AI - Introduce readers to familiar AI technologies in daily life—smart assistants, recommendation engines, and more

Artificial intelligence has quickly become a necessary tool in our daily lives, usually supporting us in the background to enhance our experiences, streamline our work, and help us make wise decisions. Once limited to the domain of science fiction or highly specialized research environments, artificial intelligence (AI) has lately found its way into almost every field of modern society. Artificial intelligence shapes our interactions from the time we wake up and check our cell phones to the way we negotiate our cities, shop online, contact one another, and get medical treatment. The ubiquity of these tools and systems driven by artificial intelligence is especially amazing; many people daily interact with them without even realizing they have done. From a futuristic concept to a technology that is both practical and ingrained, artificial intelligence (AI) quietly shapes a great range of facets of modern human life.

Although artificial intelligence finds many uses, one of the most common ones in the domain of smart devices and personal digital assistants is Voice-activated assistants, including Siri, Alexa, Google Assistant, and Cortana use natural language processing and machine learning to understand user commands, answer questions, create reminders, and run smart home systems. Thanks to these assistants, which are now rather common in modern homes, users can interact with technology in a more natural and conversational way. Thanks to artificial intelligence-powered algorithms, these systems can learn from user behaviour, change their responses, and develop over time. They thus become ever more individualized and effective. The natural integration of artificial intelligence into daily routines has transformed the way people access knowledge and interact with technology.

Particularly in the curation of material and the improvement of user experiences, artificial intelligence is rather important in the entertainment and media sectors. Artificial intelligence drives the recommendation systems found in streaming companies, including Netflix, Spotify, and YouTube. Based on users' tastes and viewing past, these systems offer recommendations for movies, TV, music, and videos. These systems use the enormous volumes of data they examine to identify trends and project the kinds of material most likely to pique each unique user's curiosity. This has led to more interesting, effective, and customized experiences for entertainment that people have. AI also finds application in the content creation itself process. Algorithms let one create art, write scripts, generate music, and even create news pieces.

One more area where artificial intelligence has transformed daily life is e-commerce. Among the several online stores using artificial intelligence to customize product recommendations, maximize pricing, and simplify customer service are Amazon, eBay, and Alibaba. Artificial intelligence algorithms track consumer browsing patterns, purchase behaviour, and preferences whenever a customer visits an online store to create product recommendations most likely to be bought by the consumer. Natural language processing-powered chatbots can process returns, answer consumer questions, and offer support around the clock. This guarantees quick help for consumers and reduces the necessity of human intervention. Artificial intelligence also enhances supply chain management and logistics, so enabling timely delivery of products and effective stocking of them. These developments have improved consumer shopping experiences as well as helped companies run more effectively in their operations.

Social media companies rely heavily on artificial intelligence to provide tailored content, filter data, and spot negative behaviour as well as to identify harmful behaviour. AI algorithms decide which pages or groups users should follow as well as make recommendations for fresh connections from the posts showing on their feeds. These systems are meant to maximize user involvement by means of the identification of the kinds of materials that are most relevant to every individual. Apart from being one of the several uses of artificial intelligence, personalizing helps to find and eliminate inappropriate or damaging content, spot false news, and stop cyberbullying. By teaching machine learning models to identify trends of abuse, hate speech, or false information, we help to create online spaces that are more responsible and safer. Nevertheless, the use of artificial intelligence in social media platforms raises questions about echo chambers, algorithmic bias, and data privacy, which in turn stimulates continuous discussions concerning the suitable governance of these technologies.

Additionally, making major progress in the domains of navigation and transportation are intelligent systems. Artificial intelligence is applied by GPS systems and navigation apps like Google Maps and Waze to examine traffic patterns, project congestion, and suggest the most effective paths. These systems depend on real-time data gathered from millions of users, satellites, and traffic traffic sensors in order to maximize the efficiency of travel. Ride-sharing companies like Uber and Lyft both use artificial intelligence for the goals of matching drivers with passengers, pricing, and arriving time estimation. The development of autonomous cars also depends critically on artificial intelligence. Combining machine learning, computer vision, and sensor fusion systems helps self-driving cars perceive their surroundings, make decisions, and negotiate safe road conditions. Many contemporary vehicles already have artificial intelligence-driven capabilities, including lane assist, adaptive cruise control, and automatic emergency braking, even if completely autonomous cars are still under development. For drivers, these characteristics increase driving convenience as well as safety.

Artificial intelligence's application in the medical field has made once unattainable treatments, diagnostic processes, and patient care choices more available. Artificial intelligence-powered diagnostic tools examine medical images, including X-rays, MRIs, and CT scans, in order to detect conditions including cancer, fractures, and neurological diseases with a great degree of precision. These instruments help doctors diagnose more quickly and precisely, so enabling better patient outcomes from their work. Artificial intelligence is also applied in predictive analytics to find people who run the danger of acquiring chronic conditions. Early intervention and the creation of individualized treatment plans are thus enabled. Chatbots and virtual health assistants can handle chores, including medical information provision, appointment scheduling, and remote patient symptom monitoring. During the COVID-19 epidemic, artificial intelligence was indispensable since it enabled tracking of the virus's spread, modelling of transmission patterns, and acceleration of vaccine research. Including artificial intelligence in healthcare not only raises the standard of treatment but also helps to solve issues with limited resources and growing patient demand.

Furthermore, artificial intelligence has helped the discipline of education since it has made it possible to offer customized learning opportunities and improved access. Artificial intelligence-powered learning systems can change material to fit the learning pace and style of every student, so offering unique instruction and feedback. Intelligent tutoring systems point up knowledge gaps, offer real-time support, and recommend activities meant especially to reinforce learning. Language learning apps like Duolingo use artificial intelligence to customize the degree of difficulty of every lesson and offer unique feedback depending on the performance of the users. Artificial intelligence analytics lets educators monitor student involvement, assess student development, spot students who might be at risk, and call for further help. Moreover, artificial intelligence tools provide speech-to-text services, automated captions, and screen readers, so enabling students with disabilities to access instructional materials. This helps to guarantee that education is fair for all and available to every student.

In the realm of financial services, where it has transformed individual's handling of their money and investments and identification of fraudulent activity, it has also become absolutely essential. Banking apps use artificial intelligence to examine spending trends, offer budgeting tips, and recommend financial plans. Robo-advisors use machine learning to create and control investment portfolios for consumers depending on their financial goals and degree of risk tolerance. Furthermore, very much used in fraud detection systems is artificial intelligence. These systems track unusual activity in transactions and either alert consumers or block dubious behaviour in real time. Artificial intelligence algorithms assess applicants' creditworthiness for lending and credit scoring by examining a broad range of data, including perhaps social behaviour, employment status, and financial history. These tools have been created to help make financial services more secure, accessible, and efficient.

Artificial intelligence has transformed customer service as companies in all kinds of fields use chatbots and virtual agents to answer questions, fix problems, and greatly raise customer satisfaction. These artificial intelligence systems can learn over time, acquire knowledge by interactions, and understand natural language. Apart from responding right away, they reduce wait times and are accessible all through the day and night. Apart from responding to regular inquiries, artificial intelligence can support human agents by means of customer sentiment analysis, response suggestions, and ranking of tickets in importance. This cooperation between people and machines produces a more efficient and responsive customer support system, which finally helps to improve the whole experience that customers have.

Within the field of agriculture, artificial intelligence is helping to maximize resource use, increase output, and advance environmentally friendly farming methods. Precision agriculture uses sensors run under artificial intelligence, drones, and imaging technologies to monitor crop health, soil conditions, and weather patterns. Real-time insights given to farmers help them to make decisions depending on data on planting, irrigation, fertilization, and pest control. AI algorithms could be able to predict crop yields, identify disease outbreaks, and suggest ideal harvesting times—all of which help to lower waste and increase efficiency. By lowering the usage of water, chemicals, and other inputs, these technologies not only enhance food security but also help to build environmentally sustainable practices.

Manufacturing and industry have embraced artificial intelligence for uses in predictive maintenance, quality control, and automation. Artificial intelligence-powered robotics can perform repeated tasks with accuracy, speed, and consistency, so enhancing production efficiency and lowering labour costs. By means of machine vision systems, product defects are inspected, preserving high standards of quality and lowering the error count. Predictive maintenance—which uses artificial intelligence—allows equipment to be watched over and signs of wear or failure found before they cause downtime. This raises operational dependability and helps to lower costs. Artificial intelligence also helps companies maximize supply chains, allowing them to more precisely project demand, control inventory, and react to changing market conditions.

Furthermore, helping to improve environmental and energy management is artificial intelligence. Smart grids use artificial intelligence to track energy consumption, balance supply, and demand, and include renewable energy sources, including solar and wind power. Utilities help artificial intelligence find flaws, boost energy efficiency, and stop blackouts. Artificial intelligence is applied in environmental monitoring to examine data gathered from satellites, sensors, and drones in order to monitor air and water quality, track deforestation, and project natural disasters. These insights enable governments, scientists, and environmentalists to act quickly to safeguard ecosystems in their particular domains. Artificial intelligence is a great tool for sustainability since it can help to solve world issues including resource depletion and climate change.

Additionally starting to show up in law and public administration are artificial intelligence uses. Legal practitioners use artificial intelligence to examine records, do legal research, and project case results. Artificial intelligence facilitates cost-cutting, administrative process simplification, and access to justice improvement. Governments are using artificial intelligence (AI) to enhance public services, examine policy effects, and spot fraud in welfare and tax systems. By means of openness, responsibility, and efficiency, these technologies enhance governance.

Within the creative sectors, artificial intelligence is enabling fresh kinds of artistic expression and innovation. Designers and artists use artificial intelligence to generate fresh ideas, enhance images, write music, and play about with new styles. Fashion designers use artificial intelligence to create tailored clothing, project trends, and simplify manufacturing. In the field of architecture, artificial intelligence offers help in areas of design optimization, energy modelling, and construction planning. By using these tools, conventional ideas of creativity are questioned and it is shown how people and machines might cooperate to push the envelope of design and art.

Although artificial intelligence finds many different uses in daily life, it also brings fresh obligations and difficulties. Concerns, including data privacy, algorithmic bias, and job displacement, must be addressed if we are to guarantee that artificial intelligence technologies are applied in an ethical and fair way. Technologists, legislators, ethicists, and the general public must cooperate to create frameworks that give human well-being, justice, and responsibility top priority if we are to develop artificial intelligence responsibly.

In essence, artificial intelligence is a tangible reality that directly affects our way of life, our employment, and our interactions with our surroundings; it is no longer a notion from the future. In many different contexts—personal assistants, predictive healthcare, smart agriculture, and autonomous vehicles—artificial intelligence (AI) enhances the convenience, efficiency, and creativity of daily life. Its impact is growing in almost every sector as technologies keep developing and get more entwined into our daily lives and should keep growing. By means of identification and understanding of these uses, we grow more informed and empowered citizens of the artificial intelligence driven world. The successful and responsible integration of artificial intelligence into society will depend on our capacity to balance innovation, ethical stewardship, and inclusiveness as this technology develops.

CHAPTER II

Foundations of Machine Learning

The Difference Between AI, Machine Learning, and Deep Learning - Clarify the hierarchy and distinctions among these commonly confused terms

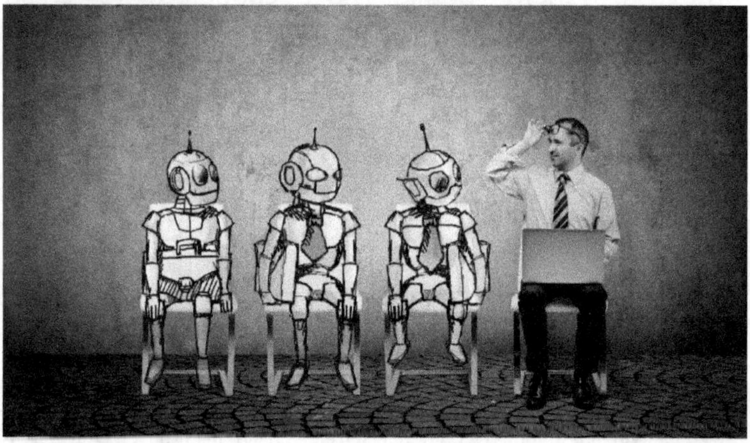

In both technical and popular language, artificial intelligence, machine learning, and deep learning are terms used often in concert. Although they are closely related and frequently cross in function and application, they are separate domains inside the larger field of computer science. Anyone trying to negotiate the world of modern technology—especially as artificial intelligence keeps invading sectors and daily life—must understand the distinctions among these three ideas. The general field of artificial intelligence is one that aims to produce systems or machines capable of completing tasks usually requiring human intelligence. Within this field, machine learning is a particular method that allows computers to learn from data and raise their performance without direct programming. Deep learning is a subset of machine learning whereby vast volumes of data are modelled and interpreted using sophisticated neural network architectures. Examining the subtleties, purposes, and roles of every one of these fields helps one to understand how they cooperate to create the technological foundation of modern intelligent systems.

Originally driven by the desire to replicate or simulate human intelligence in machines, artificial intelligence as a concept evolved. It covers a great spectrum of approaches, strategies, and objectives. Early artificial intelligence systems performed tasks using predefined rules and logic, mostly depending on Operating through if-then statements and decision trees; these rule-based systems replicated a type of logical thinking. These systems struggled with ambiguity, complexity, and dynamic input, even if they could function well in limited environments with low variables. AI developed over time to include increasingly advanced methods enabling more flexibility and performance. Artificial intelligence encompasses all, from symbolic thinking and expert systems to contemporary techniques, including machine learning and deep learning; it is not limited to one approach. Artificial intelligence seeks to produce systems with perception, reason, action, and learning ability. This covers everything from simple automation tools to more sophisticated systems understanding natural language, image recognition, strategic decision-making, and social interaction capability.

Within artificial intelligence, machine learning developed as a paradigm change. Machine learning lets computers recognize patterns and generate predictions based on data, not program machines with a set of rules. This method was motivated by the realization that experience shapes human intelligence mostly. Programmers give a machine data and let it learn for itself instead of explicitly coding every conceivable choice it could make. Machine learning's central tenet is that systems can learn from past observations and base decisions on them. Fundamentally in machine learning are algorithms including linear regression, decision trees, support vector machines, and k-nearest neighbours. Trained on datasets, these algorithms modify their internal parameters throughout this process to maximize their performance in producing predictions or classifications.

Machine learning falls mostly into three main categories: supervised, unsupervised, and reinforcement learning. In supervised learning, the method is trained on labelled data under known desired output. In a spam detection system, for instance, the algorithm is taught on emails categorized as "spam," or "not spam." It picks out elements and trends that set the two apart. Under unsupervised learning, the data lacks labels. The method looks for natural structures or groupings in the data, such as grouping consumer data depending on purchase activity. In reinforcement learning, an agent interacts with an environment, learning to make decisions by getting rewards or penalties depending on its behaviour. Robotics, gaming, and autonomous systems all use this kind of learning quite a bit. Although machine learning models can improve over time and handle difficult tasks, their capacity to generalize or grasp abstract ideas outside of the data they have been trained on is often limited.

Emerging as one of the most potent and transforming subclasses of machine learning is deep learning. The structure and purpose of the human brain—especially the network of connected neurons— inspire me. Artificial neural networks comprising layers of linked nodes, or "neurons," each processing data and passing it on to the next layer to build deep learning models. The depth of these networks distinguishes deep learning from conventional machine learning—hence the term "deep." These networks with many layers can replicate ever more intricate patterns and representations. In fields including image recognition, natural language processing, speech synthesis, and autonomous driving, deep learning has made possible breakthroughs.

Deep learning is distinguished, among other things, by its capacity to automatically extract pertinent features from unprocessed data. In conventional machine learning, a crucial first step is featuring engineering—where humans personally identify the variables most pertinent to the problem. Conversely, deep learning models can learn hierarchical representations of data, so negating the need for significant human intervention. In image recognition, for instance, early layers in a deep neural network might learn to identify edges and basic forms, while deeper layers learn to identify textures, objects, and whole scenes. For unstructured data like images, audio, and text, this automatic feature learning makes deep learning especially powerful.

Deep learning's success has been driven by several elements, including better algorithms, advances in computational capability (particularly GPUs), and the availability of vast datasets. While recurrent neural networks (RNNs) and their variants, long short-term memory (LSTM) networks, have excelled in sequence data tasks, including language translation and speech recognition, techniques, including convolutional neural networks (CNNs), have become standard for image-related tasks. More recently, the development of transformer architectures—like those behind models such as BERT and GPT—has transformed natural language processing, allowing machines to produce human-like text, summarize documents, and participate in remarkably fluid conversation.

Deep learning models are sometimes attacked for being opaque or "black boxes," notwithstanding their great power. Deep neural networks' internal workings are complex and unlike simpler machine learning algorithms, which makes it difficult to know how they get at particular decisions. Applications like healthcare, finance, or criminal justice, where responsibility and trust are absolutely vital, can find great difficulty from this lack of openness. Although methods to increase the interpretability of deep learning models are under active development by researchers, this is still a challenging and changing task.

Deep learning, artificial intelligence, and machine learning differ also in their computational and data needs. Often running with rather small datasets and limited computational resources, traditional artificial intelligence systems and simpler machine learning models can. Conversely, deep learning usually needs strong hardware and lots of data to learn properly. This reliance on data and computing capability has resulted in a concentration of deep learning research and application inside well-funded research institutes and major technology corporations. Although efforts are underway to democratize access to deep learning tools and models, smaller companies and independent developers find entrance difficult due to deep learning's resource-intensive character.

Knowing the hierarchy among artificial intelligence, machine learning, and deep learning also helps one to better define their respective scopes and constraints. The widest term for any method allowing machines to replicate human intelligence is artificial intelligence. A subset of artificial intelligence dedicated to allowing systems to learn from data is machine learning. Defined by the application of deep neural networks, deep learning is a further subset of machine learning. Every layer of this hierarchy adds more complexity and resource needs while yet building on the capacities of the one before it.

The useful applications of these technologies underline their differences and complements. Basic artificial intelligence can be found, for example, in a rule-based chatbot responding to consumer questions with preset answers. Using machine learning, a more developed chatbot learns to enhance its answers depending on user interactions. Deep learning models educated on large corpora of conversational data may be the basis of an even more sophisticated chatbot that understands context, generates human-like responses, and changes its tone and language. In the field of healthcare, too, a system that learns to predict disease risk based on patient data uses machine learning, while a diagnostic tool following a fixed decision tree evaluates symptoms and represents basic artificial intelligence. Deep learning—using convolutional neural networks trained on thousands of annotated images—may be used in a system analysing medical images to detect tumours with great accuracy.

Moreover, reflecting the larger development of intelligent systems is the changing interaction among artificial intelligence, machine learning, and deep learning. Early artificial intelligence efforts were constrained by the rigidity of rule-based approaches and the difficulties of translating human knowledge into logical rules. Machine learning brought a paradigm whereby systems could learn and adapt yet still needed major human effort in feature selection and model tuning. Deep learning has stretched the envelope by allowing end-to-end learning straight from raw data and attaining superhuman performance in jobs including image classification and language translation. Emphasizing the need for ethical and responsible development, this advancement has also raised fresh issues about bias, justice, and control.

Not only for intellectual clarity but also for pragmatic decision-making, the differences between artificial intelligence, machine learning, and deep learning will remain significant as technology develops. Understanding which tools and approaches fit various issues helps businesses, legislators, and the general public. Not every application calls for the computational intensity and complexity of deep learning; often, simpler machine learning models or even conventional artificial intelligence methods may be more successful and efficient. Selecting the appropriate strategy calls for a clear awareness of the problem domain, data availability, resource constraints, and intended results.

Moreover, the future of intelligent systems will probably involve a mix of techniques from the AI spectrum. Already under investigation to improve interpretability and generalization are hybrid models combining symbolic thinking with deep learning. Another front in deep learning is transfer learning, which lets models educated on one task be adapted to new but related tasks. Federated learning helps models to be trained across distributed devices without sharing raw data, addressing privacy issues. Though their basic differences will still define how we design, use, and interact with intelligent systems, the lines separating artificial intelligence, machine learning, and deep learning may blur as these developments take place.

All told, artificial intelligence is the great dream of machines displaying intelligent behaviour. While deep learning gives strong tools for modelling complicated patterns through neural networks, machine learning provides the means for systems to learn from data within this wide field. Every level in this hierarchy builds on the one before it provides ever more capacity at the expense of more complexity and resource demand. Understanding the variations among these three pillars of modern intelligence not only helps us to grasp how today's most advanced technologies operate but also enables us to properly and responsibly use their possibilities in a society progressively shaped by intelligent machines.

The Learning Paradigms: Supervised, Unsupervised, and Reinforcement Learning - Explain how machines learn from data using real-world analogies

Since its inception, artificial intelligence has seen amazing developments; machine learning is now a potent tool helping machines learn from data. The several learning paradigms that define how an algorithm interacts with data and generates knowledge from it define the centrality of the development and operation of machine learning systems. Among the most often used learning paradigms are reinforcement learning, unsupervised learning, and supervised learning. Reflecting many ways by which machines might approximate human-like cognition and decision-making, each of these paradigms runs under a different philosophical and methodological approach to learning. Comprehending how intelligent systems are trained, optimized, and used over a broad spectrum of pragmatic applications in sectors including healthcare, finance, marketing, robotics, and beyond depends on an awareness of these paradigms.

Among the most well-known and often applied machine learning models is probably supervised learning. It is predicated on the learning from labelled data concept, in which every training set data point corresponds with a target or correct output value. The basic concept is to give the algorithm lots of input-output pairs so it may learn a mapping from inputs to outputs. The method adjusts its internal parameters to reduce the error in its predictions by looking at the interaction between the features of the input data and the matching labels. By means of repeated exposure to the labelled data, the model develops over time to be able to generalize from the training data to generate accurate predictions on fresh, unaccustomed data. When given similar challenges, this process closely reflects how a student learns by seeing examples with known answers and attempting to duplicate those answers.

Two main chores define the extent of supervised learning: classification and regression. In classification, one wants to match input data to one of several predefined groups. Applications including spam detection, image recognition, sentiment analysis, and medical diagnosis—where the model must choose the appropriate label or class for every input—often feature this. In regression problems, the goal is to forecast an ongoing value from given data. Predicting house prices, for instance, depending on variables including location, size, and number of rooms, is a regression challenge. Depending on the type of work, the performance of the supervised learning model is assessed in both tasks using criteria including accuracy, precision, recall, mean squared error or other domain-specific assessments.

One of the main benefits of supervised learning is the availability of labelled data, providing clarity and structure. This lets performance assessments and rather simple training procedures run. This reliance on labelled data, meanwhile, also has a big drawback. Large amounts of precisely labelled data are costly, time-consuming, or absolutely impractical in many real-world situations. For disease diagnosis, for example, labelling medical images calls for both great human effort and professional knowledge. Furthermore, if the training data does not sufficiently reflect the variability and complexity of the real-world environment the supervised learning models are expected to operate, they sometimes suffer from generalization.

Unsupervised learning functions on unlabelled data, unlike supervised learning. There are neither predefined output labels nor categories for the method. Rather, it seeks by itself underlying patterns, structures, or connections inside the input data. More exploratory in character, this kind of learning aims to expose latent structures free from clear direction. In unsupervised learning, one of the main activities is clustering—that is, grouping data points depending on their similarity. Data points in every cluster are more like one another than in those of other clusters. Customer segmentation, market research, social network analysis, and image compression—all of which use this method—also depend on it.

Dimensionality reduction—that is, lowering the number of variables or features in a dataset while maintaining its fundamental information—is another important chore in unsupervised learning. Often used to translate high-dimensional data into lower-dimensional representations are techniques including t-distributed stochastic neighbour embedding (t-SNE) and principal component analysis (PCA). Particularly helpful in visualizing, noise reduction, and as a preprocessing step for other machine learning techniques are these approaches. In anomaly detection—where the model finds data points greatly outside the norm—unsupervised learning is also essential. In fault diagnosis, network security, and fraud detection especially this is quite helpful.

Unsupervised learning's ability to operate with unlabelled data—far more plentiful and simpler to acquire than labelled data—is its primary advantage. This creates chances to leverage big datasets for value extraction free from expensive labelling requirements. Unsupervised learning can also expose trends and insights not immediately obvious to human analysts. However, the absence of labels creates difficulties in assessing model performance as well. It can be challenging to ascertain whether the found trends are significant or how well the model is performing since there is no ground truth to contrast against. Unsupervised learning's success depends on domain knowledge to interpret and validate the findings most of the time.

Inspired by behavioural psychology and decision theory, reinforcement learning offers a quite different method of machine learning. Under this paradigm, an agent learns to interact with an environment in order to accomplish a given objective. Reinforcement learning is dynamic, sequential decision-making, unlike supervised learning, in which the model learns from a stationary dataset. After noting the condition of the surroundings, the agent acts and gets comments in the form of a reward or a penalty. The agent discovers over time a policy—a strategy for selecting behaviour—that optimizes the total reward. By means of this iterative process, the agent can adapt and enhance its behaviour depending on the results of its activities.

Usually, the Markov decision processes (MDPs) formalize the interaction between the agent and the environment, so guiding the reinforcement learning process. An MDP consists of the set of potential states, the set of accessible actions, the transition probabilities between states, the reward function, and the policy. The agent wants to identify the best policy that, over time, generates the maximum expected return. Applications for reinforcement learning have been effectively successful in robotics, game playing, resource management, and autonomous driving. Using often advanced techniques like deep reinforcement learning, notable successes include training agents to play challenging games, including chess, Go, and video games at superhuman levels.

Reinforcement learning is distinguished from other approaches in that it emphasizes learning by experience. The agent explores the surroundings and learns from the results of its activities; it does not need labelled data. This makes reinforcement learning especially appropriate for tasks where the right actions are unknown in advance and must be found by interaction. Still, this exploratory character presents difficulties as well. The agent might have to try several actions before finding successful strategies; thus, the learning process can be slow and sample-inefficient. Furthermore, non-trivial chores requiring careful thought are creating suitable reward systems and guaranteeing stability in learning.

Every one of these learning paradigms—supervised, unsupervised, and reinforcement learning—offers special advantages and fits various kinds of problems. Actually, the choice of paradigm relies on elements, including the type of data, the availability of labels, the difficulty of the work, and the desired results. Many real-world applications make use of hybrid methods, combining aspects of several paradigms in order to take use of their complimentary benefits. When labelled data is limited, for instance, semi-supervised learning aggregates labelled and unlabelled data to improve performance. A type of unsupervised learning, self-supervised learning, creates pseudo-labels from the data itself to equip models for supervised learning. Likewise, imitation learning—that is, combining reinforcement learning with supervised learning—can help the agent navigate with expert demonstrations.

Learning paradigms' evolution also reflects larger artificial intelligence and cognitive science trends. Supervised learning fits conventional classroom environments in which students receive examples with the right answers. Unsupervised learning reflects human curiosity and the natural capacity to find trends free from explicit direction. The core of experiential learning—where rewards and consequences shape behaviour—is captured in reinforcement learning. These paradigms are getting more complex as research develops, combining with developments in deep learning, probabilistic modelling, and neuroscience-inspired designs to produce more flexible, intelligent, and adaptive systems.

Furthermore, these learning paradigms have major social ramifications. Predictive analytics makes extensive use of supervised learning, which raises issues about fairness, bias, and responsibility when models make decisions affecting personal lives. Although unsupervised learning is great for discovery, if the underlying data shows social inequalities, it can reinforce already existing prejudices. Particularly in high-stakes situations, reinforcement learning, with its autonomous decision-making powers, presents difficulties for safety, ethical behaviour, and long-term consequences. Dealing with these problems calls for both a dedication to responsible artificial intelligence development and a thorough awareness of the strengths and constraints of every paradigm.

The need to learn its fundamental paradigms cannot be emphasized as artificial intelligence gets more ingrained in our daily lives. Whether creating medical diagnostic tools, personal assistants, self-driving cars, or recommendation engines, the learning paradigm chosen influences the behaviour, capabilities, and dependability of the produced system. To guarantee that artificial intelligence technologies effectively serve human values and needs, educators, researchers, developers, and legislators have to be endowed with a sophisticated knowledge of supervised, unsupervised, and reinforcement learning. The power of algorithms is only one aspect of intelligent systems; another is our collective wisdom on when and how to implement them. Examining the depths of these learning paradigms helps us to create machines that not only learn but also significantly help to create a more intelligent, fair, and connected world.

Data: The Fuel of AI - Highlight the role and importance of high-quality data in training intelligent systems

Many times, data is referred to as the new oil of the modern age—a basic resource running artificial intelligence engines. In the framework of artificial intelligence, data is not only a tool or a complement but rather the very lifeblood running under intelligent systems. Data is what machines learn, adapt, predict, and replicate forms of thinking that roughly reflect human cognition. From the most sophisticated neural networks to the most basic predictive models, every element of artificial intelligence is closely related to the quality, volume, and structure of the data it consumes. This interdependence between artificial intelligence and data emphasizes the critical part data performs in allowing artificial intelligence to flourish in the real world, so offering a better knowledge of why data is regarded as the fuel of AI.

Training every artificial intelligence model starts with data collecting. An algorithm is blind, aimless, and incapable of learning or developing without data. In supervised learning, for example, models are taught to identify trends and make decisions depending on past events using labelled datasets. These datasets might include numerical records marked with results, texts annotated with emotions, or images labelled with the objects they depict. Every label act as a point of reference, a lesson the model picks from which to extend to fresh, unprocessed data. Under this paradigm, the quality of the data—that which is representative, accurate, and comprehensive—determines the model's efficacy exactly. Directly compromising the performance and dependability of the resulting artificial intelligence system are poor data quality, including erroneous labels, missing values, or skewed distributions.

Though the structure and labelling may change, data remains equally vital in unsupervised learning. Here, among unlabelled data, algorithms seek hidden patterns, groups, or structures. The model depends entirely on the inherent features of the data to find significant insights, whether it is reducing the dimensionality of large datasets for visualization needs or grouping consumers with similar behaviours. The capacity of the algorithm to find pertinent groupings and connections directly depends on the richness and variety of the data. The unsupervised learning process may fail to find practical or actionable patterns without enough variability or depth, making the exercise useless.

Though it takes a more interactive form, reinforcement learning too is based on data. Unlike fixed datasets, reinforcement learning depends on data created by interactions with an environment. The experiences of the agent—states seen, actions done, rewards acquired—form a dynamic dataset changing with time. These encounters are crucial in forming the agent's awareness of its surroundings and direction toward actions maximizing long-term benefits. Every choice adds to a feedback loop, and the aggregated information gathered from many interactions helps the agent to improve its approaches. The speed and success of learning are much influenced by the accuracy and completeness of this data as well as by the consistency of the surroundings and the clarity of rewards.

Data is still absolutely vital for the deployment and maintenance of artificial intelligence systems outside of the training stage. Once operational, an artificial intelligence model needs to be constantly watched over and updated using fresh data to guarantee it stays relevant and accurate. This is especially true in dynamic fields, including financial markets, healthcare diagnostics, and autonomous driving, were conditions very quickly. Under such conditions, the original training data might become obsolete or inadequate; thus, constant data collecting and model retraining become necessary. Continuous data availability is, therefore, a must for sustainable AI performance since even the most advanced artificial intelligence systems can become obsolete or dangerous without fresh, relevant data.

The ability of data to capture the complexity and nuance of the real world adds still another level of relevance for artificial intelligence. Real-world events are often defined by subtle interdependencies, contextual variations, and uncertain signals; they are seldom simple or linear. Retaining this complexity in data form is a difficult but necessary chore. High-quality datasets must be thorough enough to include edge cases and rare events, varied enough to reflect the wide spectrum of real-world conditions, and detailed enough to enable subtle interpretations. In natural language processing, for instance, knowing human language means knowing idioms, slang, cultural references, and emotional tones. Training artificial intelligence models to understand and create language with human-like fluency calls for a large corpus of text reflecting the richness and variety of human communication.

Data in artificial intelligence also has significant and broad ethical ramifications. AI models naturally absorb the prejudices, inequalities, and biases in the data they are fed since they learn from that data. Should historical data show underrepresents of some groups or reflect discriminatory policies, the resulting artificial intelligence systems might either reinforce or even magnify these prejudices. This has been seen in many different contexts, from credit scoring systems that disadvantage particular groups to facial recognition systems that underperform on particular demographics to recruiting algorithms that favour particular profiles. Dealing with these ethical issues calls for thorough data auditing, varied data sources, and open model evaluation to make sure artificial intelligence systems advance justice and equity instead of solidifying already present inequalities.

Furthermore, the sheer volume of data needed for contemporary artificial intelligence systems raises questions about data governance, security, and privacy. Many artificial intelligence applications depend on personal information gathered via sensors, digital platforms, and other surveillance systems from individuals. One urgent issue is making sure this data is gathered morally, kept safely, and applied sensibly. In the public debate on artificial intelligence, data breaches, illegal monitoring, and abuse of private data loom big. Aiming to safeguard people's data rights, rules, including the General Data Protection Regulation (GDPR) in Europe and similar frameworks globally, restrict data collecting and mandate responsibility and openness in artificial intelligence systems. One of the main moral conundrums in the era of artificial intelligence is juggling the demand for data with the necessity to defend personal privacy.

Trustworthy artificial intelligence systems also depend critically on data provenance and quality assurance. Knowing where data comes from, how it was gathered, and under what circumstances it was labelled or structured helps one evaluates its fit for a given application. Data gathered from social media, for example, might be noisy, incomplete, or unrepresentative even while it reflects unforced, unvarnished human behaviour. Although they lack generalizability, data collected in controlled settings—such as laboratory experiments or clinical trials—may be more organized and consistent. Processes, including cleaning, normalizing, deduplication, and validation—each of which adds to the accuracy and resilience of the artificial intelligence model—help to guarantee data quality.

Big data's emergence in recent years has changed the field of artificial intelligence by allowing models to learn from datasets of hitherto unheard-of scope. In fields including computer vision, where models trained on millions of labelled images have achieved superhuman accuracy, and language modelling, where transformer-based architectures have used vast text corpora to produce remarkably coherent and contextually relevant prose, this has produced breakthroughs. Big data's advantages, meanwhile, also present a set of difficulties. Large volumes of data storage, management, and processing call for major computational resources and infrastructure, including scalable storage systems, fast networks, and powerful servers. These resource-intensive operations are under more and more environmental impact, which fuels calls for more energy-efficient data processing and model training methods.

Moreover, access to high-quality data determines in great part the democratization of artificial intelligence. Developing competitive AI systems benefits organizations and researchers with access to large datasets especially. This begs questions about data monopolies, in which a small number of tech behemoths control enormous amounts of data, so restricting chances for independent research and smaller companies. Open data initiatives, data-sharing platforms, and cooperative research projects aiming at making valuable datasets available to a larger community help to offset this disparity. By helping to level the playing field, initiatives like these promote diversity and innovation in the AI ecosystem.

Emerging as a potential solution for data shortage and privacy issues is synthetic data creation. Using algorithms to create synthetic data that replicates the statistical characteristics of real-world datasets allows developers to enhance their training data without violating private information. In sectors including healthcare and finance, where real data is highly controlled and challenging to share, synthetic data is especially helpful. Although synthetic data cannot fully replace real data, it can be a useful complement that helps to enable stronger and privacy-conscious artificial intelligence development.

Evaluating and verifying artificial intelligence systems also depends much on data. AI models have to be tested on separate validation and test datasets before they are put into use to evaluate their generalizing capacity. These datasets have to be carefully selected to guarantee they are representative and free from data leakage, in which case information from the training set unintentionally affects the evaluation outcomes. Continuous monitoring and data-driven performance evaluations are essential post-deployment to identify model drift—that is, where changes in the underlying data distribution cause the performance of the artificial intelligence system to degrade with time. This phenomenon emphasizes the dynamic character of data and the necessity of constant attention to keep artificial intelligence systems integrity.

AI's multidisciplinary character means that domain experts often must interpret and contextualize data. In medical uses, for example, knowing the subtleties of diagnostic images or patient histories calls for a professional opinion. In both legal and financial spheres, data has to be interpreted in line with ethical and legal norms. Ensuring that artificial intelligence systems are not only technically accurate but also contextually appropriate and matched with real-world needs depends on cooperation between data scientists and domain experts.

Looking ahead, the symbiotic interaction between artificial intelligence and data is expected to get ever more complex. AI technologies will progressively be involved in the creation, improvement, and analysis of data as they develop, forming feedback loops that improve the algorithms as well as the data. Active learning methods, for instance, let models choose which data points would be most useful for labelling next, so optimizing the data collecting process. Human-in-the-loop systems similarly mix algorithmic processing with human judgment to create and validate data in difficult or uncertain settings.

CHAPTER III

Building Blocks of Machine Learning Models

Features, Labels, and Datasets - Introduce the core components of any machine learning problem

The basic building blocks guiding how algorithms learn, make decisions and produce insights define artificial intelligence and machine learning at their core. Among these fundamental elements, features, labels, and datasets constitute the necessary structure via which intelligent systems understand the environment, learn patterns, and generate predictions. Not only do AI practitioners but also everyone else trying to understand how contemporary AI technologies work depend on in-depth knowledge of these ideas. These components enable algorithms in machine learning to convert unstructured data into ordered knowledge, so serving as their vocabulary. Although the terms seem technical, their conceptual roots are in basic ideas that reflect how people absorb knowledge in daily life.

In its most fundamental form, a feature is a single, quantifiable attribute or quality of a phenomenon under observation. Practically speaking, features are the inputs a machine learning model uses to complete a task. Features might include the number of bedrooms, square footage, location, and year of construction if an artificial intelligence model is taught to forecast the price of a house. Every element adds a different bit of information; taken as a whole, they create a multi-dimensional perspective of the subject matter. The performance of the model can be changed by the choice, engineering, and modification of these aspects. While poor or irrelevant features might hide patterns and reduce accuracy, good features help the model learn pertinent relationships.

Consequently, a crucial phase of the machine learning process is featuring engineering. It entails either adding fresh features or modifying current ones to improve the model's predictive capability. To record cyclical patterns in user behaviour, one might, for instance, extract the day of the week or hour of the day instead of raw timestamps. As it combines an awareness of the problem context with the mathematical rigor required to efficiently manipulate data, feature engineering calls for both domain knowledge and technical expertise. Many times, the quality of the features used as input determines a machine learning model's success more so than its algorithm's complexity.

Unlike features, labels reflect the targets or outputs a model seeks to predict. Labels in supervised learning are known results connected with every set of features. They are the responses in a set of cases the model uses for learning. Emails might be labelled as "spam" or "not spam," for example, in a spam detecting system. Every image in image classification could be tagged with the object it contains, say "cat, "dog," or "car." What the model tries to grasp is the relationship between features and labels. The model creates an internal representation or function that maps inputs to outputs by examining how variations in features match variations in labels.

The learning process is much influenced by the quality of labels. Bad generalizing to new data and misleading the model can result from erroneous, inconsistent, or vague labels. This difficulty is especially noticeable in fields like medical diagnosis or sentiment analysis, where labelling is arbitrary or calls for expert opinion. In such fields, guaranteeing the accuracy of labels usually calls for domain experts' validation or agreement among several annotators. Furthermore, important are the labels' structure and level of detail. While multi-class or multi-label systems can capture more complicated relationships at the expense of more complexity in modelling and evaluation, binary labels offer simplicity but may limit nuance.

Furthermore, defining the kind of machine learning challenges being tackled are labels. Whereas classification problems involve discrete categories or classes, regression problems entail continuous labels—such as temperature or price. While multi-label classification lets many labels be assigned to a single instance, multi-class classification is selecting among several classes. Knowing the type of labels helps one choose the suitable evaluation measures, loss functions, and algorithms. For balanced classification problems, for instance, accuracy might be sufficient, but imbalanced labels usually call for accuracy, recall, or F1-score to be more fairly represent performance.

Features and labels abound in datasets, the ordered sets of examples supporting training, validation, and testing of machine learning models. Rows, each standing for a unique example, make up a dataset; columns for features and labels follow from the dataset, exposing the algorithm to patterns, anomalies, correlations, and noise, so capturing its whole learning environment. Machine learning models iteratively improve by means of repeated exposure to this ordered data, so optimizing their internal parameters to reduce error and maximize predictive performance.

Small, carefully selected collections fit for experimentation to massive corpora used in large-scale industrial applications—datasets come in many forms and sizes. The capacity of the model to efficiently generalize depends on the dataset size. Small datasets might not be enough to detect intricate trends or might cause overfitting—that is, where the model memorizes rather than learns. Large datasets, on the other hand, can enable the training of advanced models, including deep neural networks, but demand careful management and major computational resources. Oftentimes, a dataset's quality, variety, and representativeness exceed its sheer volume. Inaccurate or unfair results can result from a sizable skewed, biased, or redundant dataset.

Data collecting, cleaning, annotation, and partitioning are just a few of the several important phases in which datasets are built. Data collecting is compiling unprocessed data from many sources—including sensors, databases, user interactions, or web scraping. Many times, this raw data includes mistakes, duplicates, missing values, or inconsistencies. By means of imputation, normalizing, and outlier removal, data cleaning solves these problems so guaranteeing a consistent and reliable dataset. Usually requiring human intervention or automated tools, annotations add the required labels or metadata. To support strong model development and evaluation, partitioning finally separates the dataset into training, validation, and test sets.

The training set is the part of the data used to teach the model the correlations between labels and features. The model learns its parameters and shapes its internal representation via this subset. A checkpoint for hyperparameter tuning, model comparison, and overfit monitoring is the validation set. It provides a preview of the generalizing capacity of the model on the unavailability of data. Held apart from the training process, the test set offers an objective assessment of the actual performance of the model. Analysing the model on this last set will help developers determine its likely performance in manufacturing settings.

In many real-world situations, datasets might show imbalance—that is, underrepresentation of some classes or outcomes. In disciplines including fraud detection or disease diagnosis, where positive cases are rare relative to negatives, this is typical. For model training, imbalanced datasets provide major difficulties since algorithms could grow biased toward majority classes, so neglecting the minority. Resampling, synthetic data generation, and class weighting are among the methods used to balance this disparity and guarantee that the model gives rare but significant events enough consideration.

Since the data used to train artificial intelligence systems directly affects their behaviour, fairness, and societal impact, ethical issues in dataset development and application take first priority. Biassed datasets can produce discriminating results, so supporting already existing disparities and marginalizing underprivileged groups. Applications, including predictive policing, hiring systems, and facial recognition, have seen this as well. Datasets must be kept fair by intentional efforts to include varied populations, check for representational biases, and do impact studies. Building trust in artificial intelligence systems and reducing possible risks depend on open methods of gathering, labelling, and using datasets.

Another essential aspect of dataset handling is privacy. Many datasets—especially those involving personal data—carry hazards of re-identification, misuse, or illegal access. Legal systems, including the General Data Protection Regulation (GDPR), underline the need for data minimization, informed permission, and data anonymizing. Differential privacy, federated learning, and homomorphic encryption are among the methods meant to safeguard personal data while yet allowing effective model training. A difficult but necessary task in the ethical growth of artificial intelligence is juggling the demand for data with the right to privacy.

Improving model efficiency and interpretability depends much on the idea of feature selection. Not every feature adds equally to predictive power; some may be useless, redundant, or even dangerous. While discarding the rest, feature selection techniques—both statistical and algorithmic—help determine the most informative ones. Eliminating noise lowers the dataset's dimensionality, accelerates training, and often increases generalization. Moreover, fewer features make the model simpler to grasp, which is especially important in high-stakes fields like healthcare or finance, where knowledge of the justification behind decisions is absolutely vital.

Especially in deep learning, automated feature extraction has transformed the way that features are derived from raw data. For example, convolutional neural networks automatically learn spatial hierarchies of features from images, so removing the need for hand feature engineering. Analogous learning of temporal and contextual features from text and sequences guides recurrent and transformer-based models. These methods push the envelope of what artificial intelligence systems can accomplish by letting models find abstract representations that might be challenging for humans to define explicitly. Still, given their often high-dimensional, non-intuitive nature, such characteristics remain difficult to interpret.

Datasets change with time as well, particularly in dynamic settings where trends alter. Long-term model dependability suffers from these phenomena sometimes known as concept drift. Models educated on past data may become obsolete or inaccurate as the relationship between features and labels changes. Dealing with concept drift calls for both retraining and constant monitoring as well as adaptation. Models are kept in line with present reality by means of real-time data pipelines and incremental learning algorithms: Ignoring changing data might result in performance drops and mistrust of artificial intelligence systems.

Datasets are routinely shared among companies, researchers, or across geographical distances in cooperative environments. This brings difficulties with provenance, interoperability, and standardizing. Effective cooperation depends on consistent formatting of datasets, annotations using common taxonomies, and accompaniment with metadata. Tracking data lineage—that is, the source, changes, and use of data—improves responsibility and openness. Open datasets, benchmarks, and repositories all help to democratize data and support repeatable research.

Features, labels, and datasets will evolve toward ever more automation, intelligence, and integration. By letting models learn from unprocessed data using internal signals, advances in self-supervised learning seek to lower reliance on labelled data. Likewise, developments in active learning let models choose the most instructive examples to label, so optimizing data annotation activities. Large, task-specific datasets are less needed since transfer learning and domain adaptation allow the reuse of features and models across several but connected datasets.

In artificial intelligence and machine learning, features, labels, and datasets are essentially the fundamental components. Through which algorithms get knowledge and generate predictions, they stand for the inputs, outputs, and learning environments. Strong, fair, and efficient artificial intelligence systems depend on mastery of these ideas. Their design, quality, and ethical behaviour define not only technical performance but also social influence. Understanding and appreciating the power of data becomes a responsibility shared by all stakeholders—developers, researchers, legislators, and citizens alike—as artificial intelligence keeps invading every sphere of modern life. Not only will algorithms define the direction of artificial intelligence, but also the care and consideration with which we handle the data guiding them.

Training, Validation, and Testing - Walk through how models are trained and evaluated using split datasets

The lifetime of creating machine learning and artificial intelligence models depends critically on training, validation, and testing. In practical applications, these phases guarantee that a model not only learns from data but also generalizes effectively to new, unseen inputs and preserves dependability and accuracy. Separating data into training, validation, and testing sets gives the learning process structure and helps to prevent common problems, including underfitting and overfitting, while fairly evaluating a model's ability. Every phase has a different function and is essential in guiding the model from the first development stage until deployment and actual application.

The central learning happens during the training phase. A model is exposed to a dataset, including labelled examples, during this phase, from which it learns the underlying relationships between input features and their corresponding outputs. Often in the form of mathematical functions, these examples help the model create internal representations that let it approximate results for like inputs. The training process consists of iterative algorithms optimizing parameters to minimize a selected loss function—a mathematical expression expressing the error between the true labels and the predicted values. The type of model will determine whether this process applies gradient descent, backpropagation, or probabilistic inference. The model progressively increases its capacity to precisely map inputs to outputs as it gathers more data and modulates its parameters.

Training accuracy by itself, meanwhile, is not a good gauge of a model's performance. A model that performs very well on training data could just be memorizing the patterns in the dataset instead of grasping generally applicable rules. Overfitting is the phenomenon whereby models are highly tuned to the details of the training data but perform poorly on fresh inputs. The validation set is a different collection of data used to handle this. Acting as a proxy for unseen data, the validation set aids in evaluating the generalization of the model throughout the training process. Evaluating model performance on the validation set helps developers to identify overfitting and modify several hyperparameters, including learning rate, number of layers, regularization techniques, and batch size, so balancing the fitting of the training data with maintaining generalizability.

For hyperparameter tuning and model selection especially, the validation phase is quite crucial. The validation set provides a consistent framework for comparing the relative performance of several models or configurations since several may be taken into consideration during development. Depending on the work, it offers a feedback loop whereby developers may iteratively improve their models depending on objective criteria, including accuracy, precision, recall, or area under the ROC curve. Sometimes sophisticated methods like k-fold cross-valuation—where the validation process is repeated across several dataset partitions to guarantee resilience and lower evaluation variance—are applied. When data is limited, this approach is especially helpful since it lets one evaluate more completely without compromising too much training data.

Testing comes last once a model has been trained and validated since it offers a fair assessment of its performance. Data not used during training or validation makes up the test set, so guaranteeing that the model is exposed to totally fresh data. This is vital since it mimics actual deployment, in which case the model will be expected to generate forecasts on data it has never encountered. Revealing strengths, shortcomings, and possible limits, the performance on the test set offers a reasonable projection of how the model will behave in manufacturing surroundings. A notable decline in accuracy between the test and validation sets could point to hidden biases not taken into consideration during validation or data leakage—that is, information from the test set unintentionally affected the training process.

First and most important is the integrity of the testing process. To avoid overfitting the test data, it should be carried out just once per finalized model. Testing and modifying the model repeatedly depending on test performance transforms the test set into a de facto validation set, so compromising its objective as an objective assessor. Many companies use holdout datasets, blind testing, and third-party validation to guarantee credibility and so preserve the objectivity of the testing process. Test sets are sometimes kept secret until final entries in competitive settings and research challenges in order to prevent over-optimization or manipulation.

Fundamental to machine learning, the careful division of data into training, validation, and test sets can vary depending on the task, the type of data, and the aims of the analysis. In some fields, chronological data—such as time series or event logs—demand that training comes before validation, which then comes before testing, preserving the natural flow of events to prevent data leakage. Stratified sampling guarantees, in other situations, particularly with unbalanced or rare events, that each subset of data preserves the same class distribution as the original dataset, so supporting fair and representative training and evaluation.

Practical applications sometimes complicate this idealized separation by means of real-world restrictions. In medical diagnosis, for instance, labelled data could be rare and costly to acquire, making reserving enough data for validation and testing challenging. Under such conditions, semi-supervised learning, data augmentation, and transfer learning—creative ideas used to maximize limited data—are applied. Reducing the need for vast training examples, transfer learning lets a model pre-trained on a large dataset be fine-tuned on a smaller, domain-specific dataset. By means of transformations, including rotations, cropping, or noise, data augmentation synthetically increases the variety of the training set, thus improving generalization.

Moreover, the training-validation-testing paradigm has to be modified in dynamic or non-stationary settings whereby data changes over time. This difficulty, sometimes referred to as concept drift, results in changing relationships between features and outputs, so reducing the efficacy of models built on past data. Online learning and incremental training strategies then enable models to be constantly updated as fresh data arrives, so preserving their relevance and accuracy. Under such circumstances, regular re-evaluation employing revised validation and test sets becomes essential to track performance decline and start retraining cycles.

Modern artificial intelligence development makes increasing use of automation of the training, validation, and testing pipelines. Built-in capabilities for data partitioning, model training, and evaluation abound from tools and frameworks, including TensorFlow, PyTorch, and Scikit-learn. More advanced systems offer end-to-end solutions comprising hyperparameter optimization, model tracking, and performance visualization. Along with hastening progress, these instruments encourage reproducibility, openness, and team cooperation. Machine learning operations (MLOps) techniques have evolved in production settings to standardize process control models across their lifetime and link them with deployment systems for ongoing monitoring and continuous delivery.

Though it offers a strong basis for machine learning, the training-validation-testing paradigm has certain limits. In fast-changing fields, the presumption that a stationary division of data will be appropriate over time might not hold. Furthermore, depending on labelled data suggests the availability of accurate annotations, which is not always possible. In some fields, such as unsupervised learning or reinforcement learning, the definitions of training and testing vary greatly. In reinforcement learning, for example, the agent learns from interactions with an environment instead of from labelled examples; testing might thus involve assessing the agent's performance on several tasks or environments. Without labels in unsupervised learning, the emphasis moves to clustering, dimensionality reduction, or anomaly detection, so calling for different evaluation techniques.

Beyond accuracy, the training-validation-testing system has to take into account explainability, justice, and responsibility. A model that shows good statistical performance may still generate biased results or act erratically in edge situations. While explainable artificial intelligence (XAI) approaches give insights into the decision-making process, helping users and stakeholders understand why a model made a particular prediction, justice-aware learning integrates justice constraints into the training process, thus mitigating these risks. Beyond accuracy, evaluation criteria must include fairness scores, confusion matrices, and model confidence levels to guarantee that models are not only reliable but also responsible.

The rigor of the training-validation-testing system becomes especially important in safety-critical applications, including autonomous driving, healthcare, or financial systems. Errors in these fields might have serious repercussions and call for thorough testing under many demanding conditions. Robustness tests, adversarial testing, and simulations help to guarantee that models can resist attacks and real-world variation. Further stressing the need for careful and open evaluation, regulatory standards may call for formal verification, audit trails, and explainability to get acceptance for deployment.

Techniques like model ensemble and stacking—where several models are trained independently, and their predictions merged to increase performance—have attracted increasing attention in recent years. These methods gain from variety among models but must be carefully validated to avoid overfitting the validation set. Likewise, meta-learning—that is, learning to learn—involves training models across several tasks using demanding complex validation methods guaranteeing generalization and transferability. The approaches for training, validation, and testing have to change as artificial intelligence systems get more complicated and multifarious to fit fresh paradigms and demands.

The success of an artificial intelligence model is ultimately not limited by its test score or training accuracy. Its performance in real-world environments—that which is transparent, reasonable, and consistent—means what counts. The framework for training, validation, and testing offers a disciplined path to reach this objective. It arranges the learning process, prevents mistakes, and provides checkpoints for important thought and development. These fundamental ideas are still absolutely essential as the field of artificial intelligence develops since they anchor innovation in a thorough approach and responsible development in strict methodology. Though the future will surely bring fresh tools, methods, and paradigms, the core of reliable artificial intelligence will always be careful training, careful validation, and rigorous testing.

From Model to Insight: Predictions and Interpretability - Discuss how models make predictions and the importance of understanding their decisions

From the moment a machine learning model is trained, tested, and ready for use, its actual value resides not only in its predictions but also in the insights those predictions produce and the openness with which they are presented. In the present environment of artificial intelligence, where models are widely utilized to guide decisions in domains including healthcare, finance, law, education, and beyond, the capacity to comprehend a model's outputs has become just as crucial as their predicted accuracy. From a trained model to meaningful insight, the path is one of complex knowledge about how the model performs, the settings in which it is used, and the consequences of its predictions for human decision-makers. Interpretability connects the human need for intelligible, reliable, and actionable knowledge with the technical foundations of artificial intelligence.

Fundamentally, a machine learning model is a mathematical construction meant to approximate intricate relationships inside data. Once taught, it may generate predictions depending on fresh data. These forecasts might be anything from determining whether an email is spam, projecting quarterly income for a business, identifying an illness based on patient data, or suggesting a movie to a user. But unless accompanied by background explaining how the model arrived at that conclusion and why it can be believed, a raw prediction like "positive" or "95% likelihood of default" has minimal practical worth. Decision-makers in many high-stakes applications need thinking, justification, and openness in addition to the result. This is where interpretability helps people explore the black box of artificial intelligence and grasp the underlying processes of its decisions.

Several elements motivate the necessity of interpretability. First, there is the trust question. Particularly when those results have major ramifications, people are instinctively dubious of systems that generate results without providing reasons. A model that advises a certain medical treatment or rejects a loan application has to go beyond only generating a score; it also has to offer a justification that meets ethical, legal, and emotional standards. Second, interpretability helps responsibility. Tracing and clarifying decisions made by algorithms impacting people's lives becomes crucial to guarantee they are free from bias, discrimination, or error. Third, interpretability helps in improvement and debugging. Knowing why a model generates particular predictions helps developers improve performance, fix mistakes, and hone their creation.

Depending on the type of work and the model architecture, predictions from artificial intelligence models manifest themselves in numerous forms. In classification problems, the model generates a category or class label, usually together with a confidence score. In regression problems, the model forecasts an ongoing value. Whereas in natural language processing, the result can be a series of words or phrases, in recommendation systems, it might be a ranked list of items. Although these forecasts have different structures, the idea is the same: forecasts should be understandable to people who apply them. Deep learning models, which have many linked layers of neurons processing data in ways that are difficult to follow directly, present very problematic interpretability. These models can achieve amazing performance, but they sometimes give up openness for complexity.

There are two main forms of efforts to improve interpretability: intrinsic and post hoc interpretability. By nature, intrinsically interpretable models are transparent. Decision trees, linear regression, and rule-based systems—which let consumers follow a logical, explicit path from input to output—are among the examples here. Although these models are sometimes simpler to grasp and explain, they might not have the predictive ability of more sophisticated ones. Conversely, post hoc interpretability relates to models that are not naturally interpretable, such as support vector machines, neural networks, and ensemble models. Methods in this group seek to explain the behaviour of the model following training and application.

Features significance scores—which measure the effect of every input variable on the model's predictions—are among the most often utilized post hoc interpretability techniques. Tools like LIME (Local Interpretable Model-agnostic Explanations) and SHAP (Shapley Additive exPlanations) let users roughly estimate the contribution of every feature in a specific prediction. These instruments create an interpretable picture of the decision-making process by perturbing the input data and tracking how changes affect the output. In a credit scoring model, for example, SHAP values might reveal that a recent default had a negative impact on an applicant's creditworthiness while a high income and extensive credit history contributed favourably.

Visualization is also another essential aspect of interpretability. Visualization methods let human intuition access difficult model results. For image classification tasks, for instance, saliency maps or Grad-CAM might point up portions of the image most important for the prediction of the model. Attention heatmaps in natural language models indicate when producing a response or classification, which words the model concentrated most on. These graphic tools provide a window into the logical reasoning of the model that is both understandable and instructive, therefore helping non-technical stakeholders to communicate insights.

In feature engineering and model improvement, interpretability is also quite important. Knowing which features are driving predictions helps developers modify the input data to increase accuracy and resilience. They might find that some variables are redundant, pointless, or biased, which would guide judgments about data cleansing, transformation, or augmentation. Sometimes interpretability shows that a model depends on false correlations—relationships found in the training data but not relevant or dependable in use in practice. For instance, a model taught to identify pneumonia in chest X-rays may unintentionally learn to correlate the existence of a specific hospital watermark with a greater risk of sickness instead of paying attention to the medical image content itself. Without interpretability tools, such defects might be undetectable until they lead to actual mistakes.

Interpretability is not only a desired quality in regulated sectors; often, it is also a legal need. European rules like the General Data Protection Regulation (GDPR) mandate the "right to explanation," therefore empowering people to have knowledge of how automated decisions impacting them are made. In financial services, authorities need open models with audit and justification capability. Before including model outputs in diagnostic or treatment processes, clinical practitioners in healthcare have to know and trust them. These expectations have spurred the creation of explainable artificial intelligence models that incorporate openness into every phase of model development—from data collecting to model deployment and evaluation.

Moving from model to insight requires not only elucidating individual predictions but also overall comprehension of model behaviour. Analysing how the model performs over the whole dataset and seeing broad trends, decision limits, and model sensitivity helps one to achieve global interpretability. It clarifies issues like: Does the model fairly handle many demographic groups? Exist data thresholds or breakpoints that greatly affect forecasts? Does the model resist hostile or noisy inputs? Partial dependence graphs, which highlight the marginal impact of a characteristic on the expected outcome, and model summary visualizations ranking features by total relevance provide tools for global interpretability.

Furthermore, knowledge from artificial intelligence models transcends the direct use for which they are developed. Sometimes, models find fresh trends or linkages in data that inspire fresh scientific research or business plans. Models examining genomic data, for instance, could find hitherto identified gene connections connected to specific disorders. Retail models could spot new consumer trends guiding marketing initiatives. In these situations, the model serves as a catalyst for insight transcending mere prediction, therefore fostering creativity and domain-based research.

Although most people view interpretability and prediction as a trade-off—more accurate models are less interpretable—this dichotomy is being tested by continuous study in explainable artificial intelligence. New designs and training strategies are under development to strike a compromise between the demand for openness and the strength of intricate models. In natural language processing, for instance, attention-based models provide interpretable attention mechanisms together with great performance. Modular neural networks also divide difficult tasks into smaller, more comprehensible parts. Achieving both accuracy and interpretability as the field develops makes it more and more feasible, which lets artificial intelligence operate not as an enigmatic oracle but as a cooperative instrument enhancing human intelligence.

Interpretability is fundamental in human-centred artificial intelligence for efficient cooperation between people and robots. To apply AI models, users must be aware of their strengths and constraints. This includes adjusting expectations, acknowledging ambiguity, and knowing when to yield to personal opinion. Techniques for uncertainty quantification, confidence intervals, and prediction probability serve to convey the dependability of forecasts and, hence, promote responsible use. Models can also be made to flag unclear or vague situations for human inspection, hence generating a hybrid system combining the speed of automation with the subtlety of human thought.

The debate of model insight and interpretability also revolves around ethical issues. Ensuring that decisions made by AI systems in settings that impact people's lives are fair, inclusive, and free from damaging prejudice becomes very crucial. By showing how models treat various populations and whether some features disproportionately affect results, interpretability tools can help identify and reduce bias. Whereas post hoc audits evaluate the ethical consequences of model behaviour, fairness-aware learning includes fairness requirements in the modelling process. Encouragement of transparency helps interpretability to become a means of ethical responsibility in artificial intelligence.

The conversion of forecasts into practical insights becomes a strategic issue as companies apply AI models in operational environments more and more. AI-derived insights may direct decisions, streamline procedures, customize experiences, and create value in many sectors. From prediction to action, nevertheless, the road is not straightforward; it calls for human interpretation, domain expertise, and contextual awareness. Raw model results and important, informed decisions are bridged by interpretability. Knowing that the reasoning behind AI recommendations is logical and understandable helps consumers to trust and act confidently on them.

All told the path from model to insight captures the change of technical outputs into useful knowledge. Along with creating accurate forecasts, it entails confirming, contextualizing, and explaining those predictions in ways that matter to people. Interpretability guarantees that artificial intelligence systems reflect human ideals are transparent, and are under control. It builds confidence, encourages moral behaviour, helps to always improve, and lets artificial intelligence realize its full potential to influence human decisions. The capacity to transform complicated models into intelligible and practical insights will be the secret to releasing their actual power and guaranteeing that their advantages will be shared fairly and widely as artificial intelligence keeps invading all spheres of existence.

CHAPTER IV

Algorithms that Power AI

Decision Trees, Linear Regression, and k-Nearest Neighbors - Break down intuitive and foundational algorithms

Among the most fundamental algorithms in machine learning, decision trees, linear regression, and k-Nearest Neighbors each have special advantages and best applications. Early in the study of artificial intelligence, these algorithms are taught often because of their conceptual clarity and practical relevance. They enable a strong knowledge of how machines learn from data, how predictions are generated, and how several approaches might fit various kinds of situations. These algorithms' interpretability, efficiency, and simplicity—despite their apparent simplicity relative to deep learning models—have helped them to be extensively applied in both academic and commercial environments.

Determination Among the most straightforward models applied in regression and classification problems are trees. The name itself captures the way the method works—it uses feature values to separate data into branches, much like a flowchart would do. Every internal node stands for a choice on an attribute; every branch shows the result of that choice; every leaf node shows a class label or output value. Decision trees are especially interpretable since this hierarchical framework reflects human decision-making. Building a decision tree is the act of determining, at each node, the attributes that most split the data depending on criteria such as information gain or Gini impurity. These measures assess a given feature's ability to either lower uncertainty or separate the classes. The model divides the input recursively until it meets terminal circumstances, including either a preset tree depth or pure leaves.

Decision trees have one of the main benefits in their capacity to replicate intricate, nonlinear relationships in the data without any feature scaling or modification. They easily manage both numerical and categorical data and record interactions between features. Moreover, supporting missing values and somewhat resistant to outliers are decision trees. They do, however, overfit, particularly when the tree is developed too deep, catching noise rather than braidable patterns. Usually used to address this problem are pruning methods, which entail cutting off sections of the tree that have little effect on prediction accuracy. More sophisticated ensemble techniques, such as Random Forests and Gradient Boosting Machines, which aggregate several trees to boost performance, also originate in decision trees.

By representing the relationship between variables via a linear equation, Linear Regression provides a fundamentally different approach than the rule-based structure of decision trees. Mostly utilized for regression problems—where the aim is to forecast a continuous target variable—this method Assumed by linear regression is a linear combination of input elements, each multiplied by a coefficient denoting their weight or significance. Usually, by means of ordinary least squares, the model seeks the best-fitting line—that is, hyperplane in higher dimensions—that minimizes the difference between the expected and actual values.

Simple and interpretable, linear regression is among the most often used and well-known methods in statistical learning. A linear model's coefficients offer direct information on the contribution each feature makes to the prediction. For a model forecasting house prices, for example, the coefficient for square footage indicates, all else being equal, how much the price rises with each extra square foot. For exploratory data analysis and hypothesis testing, this transparency makes linear regression a great weapon. Moreover, it works well when the data satisfies hypotheses, including homoscedasticity, independence, and normality of residuals, and when the link between inputs and outputs is almost linear.

Linear regression has restrictions even if it has strengths. It battles nonlinear relationships until modified variables or polyn factors are included. It is also sensitive to multicollinearity, in which densely connected input features could skew the estimations of the model and lower interpretability. Furthermore, unless extended by logistic regression or other generalized linear models, linear regression is not very appropriate for classification problems. Still, its mathematical simplicity and usefulness make it a pillar of the basis for statistics and machine learning.

Based on the theory that comparable inputs should produce similar outputs, k-Nearest Neighbors (k-NN) presents even another view on prediction. This non-parametric, instance-based learning system memorizes rather than learns an explicit model from the training data. Based on a distance metric such as Euclidean distance, the algorithm searches for the 'k' closest points in the training data, then generates a prediction based on the majority class (for classification) or the average value (for regression) among those neighbors when a new data point requires classification or assignment of a value. Particularly in instances where the decision boundary is highly irregular or complicated, this method is amazingly simple and usually successful.

K-NN has strength in simplicity and adaptability. As long as a relevant distance metric can be established, it can adjust to almost any type of data. It fits linear and nonlinear situations since it does not assume any certain form for the decision boundary. It can also easily manage multi-class classification chores. But k-NN's simplicity comes with computational and pragmatic concessions. Especially on big datasets, it can be slow and memory-intensive since it depends on computing distances to all training samples at prediction time. The choice of "k" and the distance metric also significantly influences performance; these frequently need extensive tuning and cross-validation.

The curse of dimensionality is still another difficulty for k-NN. The idea of distance becomes less important as the number of characteristics rises; all points tend to become equidistant, therefore lowering the discriminative power of the algorithm. Many times used to solve this issue are feature selection and dimensionality reduction methods including Principal Component Analysis (PCA). Furthermore, susceptible to irrelevant or noisy characteristics is k-NN as, except from weighted or scaled correctly, all features equally affect the distance computation. Notwithstanding these constraints, k-NN continues to be a useful tool for its simplicity of use, interpretability, and adaptability to many fields like image classification, recommendation systems, and pattern identification.

These three methods—decision trees, linear regression, and k-Nearest Neighbors—showcase the variety of techniques available in machine learning. From the data they reflect several learning philosophies: functional approximation in linear regression, rule-based reasoning in decision trees, and similarity-based inference in k-NN. Every has benefits and disadvantages; the type of the problem, the data format, and the particular objectives of the analysis will determine which of them to choose. Many times, these are basic models that offer a standard for more advanced approaches. Their interpretability makes them also useful in fields where openness and explainability are essential.

Knowing these algorithms helps students and professionals to evaluate data, create models, and come to important decisions. Through their branching logic and well-defined decision paths, decision trees provide insights. A quantitative knowledge of the interactions between variables is given by linear regression. K-Nearest Neighbors allows simple, instance-based forecasts reflecting human pattern recognition. All taken together, they create a basic toolkit for every future data scientist or machine learning engineer.

Moreover, in hybrid systems and ensemble techniques, these models sometimes go well together. Random forests, for instance, allow one to join decision trees in order to lower variance and enhance generalization. In more sophisticated pipeline models where, linear trends are isolated from residual nonlinear patterns, linear regression might be a component. In systems needing strong interpretability or anomaly detection, k-NN can be a fallback. Their value is further extended by their interaction with model evaluation criteria, cross-validation, and feature engineering.

The fundamental ideas buried in these algorithms remain applicable as machine learning develops. They provide a foundation for ideas such as model interpretability, overfitting, generalization, and bias-variance trade-offs. They also provide points of access to more thorough investigations of real-world applications, statistical theory, and algorithmic design. Decision Trees, Linear Regression, and k-Nearest Neighbors remain vital in transforming unprocessed data into useful knowledge, whether it is for customer attrition, disease diagnosis, image classification, or knowledge of economic patterns.

These algorithms are educational techniques in education that assist in closing the distance between theory and practice. They let students see the impact of data quality on model performance, understand coefficients, and picture decision limits. Their quite modest computational needs make them perfect for learning and experimentation. In business, they are still preferred answers for issues where cheap overhead, fast insights, and model transparency rule most importantly. These interpretable models become even more important as regulatory systems change to reflect explainable artificial intelligence.

Ultimately, k-Nearest Neighbors, Linear Regression, and Decision Trees all represent basic concepts about how machines could learn from data and provide predictions. Its simplicity accentuates its accessibility, interpretability, and ongoing relevance rather than lessening its potency. They are the basic blocks from which more sophisticated algorithms are created and comprehended. These venerable algorithms are still essential tools for comprehending, developing, and making wise judgments in the digital age as artificial intelligence shapes our planet.

Neural Networks and Deep Learning - Introduce the basics of how neural networks work, using practical analogies

Forming the backbone of many of the most advanced and human-like AI systems already in use, neural networks and deep learning are among the most transforming ideas in the field of artificial intelligence. Image recognition, natural language processing, speech synthesis, game-playing, autonomous systems, and many more disciplines have been made possible by these technologies, transforming how machine's view, understand, and interact with data. Examining both their theoretical underpinnings and the useful applications that have brought neural networks and deep learning front stage helps one to appreciate their enormous influence.

The motivation derived from the human brain drives neural networks from their core. Artificial neural networks, however much simplified, are meant to replicate the communication style of organic neurons. Layers of linked nodes, or "neurons," each carrying a basic calculation, make up an artificial neural network. An input layer, one or more hidden layers, and an output layer comprise these neurons' arrangement. Data entered into the network moves through layers whereby every neuron uses a mathematical operation on the weighted sum of its inputs. These weights learn during the training process and define the strength of the connections, hence reducing the error between the expected and real outputs. The brilliance of this structure is in its capacity to stack several layers of these computations, approximating intricate, nonlinear functions.

Training a neural network is optimizing performance by changing the weights of the links between neurons. Usually, this is accomplished by backpropagation mixed with a gradient descent-style optimization method. By using the chain rule of calculus, backpropagation computes the gradient of the loss function with regard to every weight, therefore quantifying the influence of a tiny change in weight on the general error. Then, gradient descent iteratively modifies the weights in the direction that lowers the error using this information. By means of several iterations across a dataset, the network "learns" the embedded patterns in the data, therefore enabling accurate predictions or classifications on fresh, unknown cases.

Although shallow neural networks with one hidden layer can replicate a range of tasks, they frequently fail to capture complex patterns in high-dimensional data. Here is where deep learning—a subfield of machine learning derived from deep neural networks with many hidden layers—comes into play. Deep learning models can develop hierarchical representations of data, in which each next layer catches even more abstract characteristics. In picture recognition, for instance, the first layer would find edges, the second layer might identify forms, the third layer might find object components, and the last layer could set apart whole things. Deep networks can use this layered learning strategy to generalize from data in a manner shallow models cannot.

Particularly adapted for handling grid-like input such as photographs, the Convolutional Neural Network (CNN) is among the most powerful architectures in deep learning. CNNs use convolutional layers that apply filters to particular areas of the input, therefore leveraging the spatial structure of images. These filters learn to identify edges, textures, and shapes, therefore serving as feature detectors. By shrinking the spatial dimensions of the data, pooling layers help to create a more efficient and invariant network free from minor translation in the input. At the end of the network, fully connected layers are classified based on convolutional layer extracted features. Often outpacing human accuracy on standardized datasets, CNNs have set new performance benchmarks in picture classification, object detection, facial recognition, and other vision-related tasks.

Designed to manage sequential data like time series, text, or speech, another innovative architecture is the recurrent neural network (RNN). RNNs have loops that let data linger over time steps, unlike feedforward networks, therefore allowing them to record temporal dependencies and context. Standard RNNs thus have problems in practice that restrict their capacity to learn long-term dependencies: disappearing and ballooning gradients. More complex variations, including Long Short-Term Memory (LSTM) networks and Gated Recurrent Units (GRUs), have been created to solve these issues. These designs provide gating systems to control information flow, therefore enabling the network to save pertinent data across extended sequences. Tasks, including language modelling, machine translation, speech recognition, and music synthesis, have benefited much from RNNs and their variants.

The Transformer architecture and attention processes have driven even more progress in the field of deep learning recently. When making predictions, attention lets a model dynamically weigh the significance of various input elements while concentrating on the most significant bits. Transformers employ self-attention techniques to represent dependencies over whole sequences in parallel, therefore eliminating recurrence entirely. Large-scale language models, including BERT, GPT, and T5—which have shown amazing aptitude in comprehending and producing human-like text—have evolved from this invention. Achieving state-of-the-art results in natural language processing and creation, these models are pre-trained on vast datasets and fine-tuned for certain applications.

Large datasets and strong computational resources—especially Graphics Processing Units (GPUs) and specialized hardware like Tensor Processing Units (TPUs)—have plenty of bearing on the performance of deep learning. To prevent overfitting and to generalize effectively to new cases, training deep networks calls for large volumes of data. Furthermore, the computational needs of training millions or even billions of parameters call for parallel processing capability offered by GPUs. Further democratizing access to these potent tools, advances in cloud computing, and the creation of effective deep learning frameworks, including TensorFlow, PyTorch, and Keras, allow researchers and practitioners all around to experiment, innovate, and scale deep learning model deployment.

Neural networks and deep learning models have difficulties, notwithstanding their remarkable power. Their opacity, sometimes known as the "black box" issue, raises serious questions about why a model chose a given course of action. In high-stakes applications like healthcare, finance, or criminal justice, where knowledge of the reasoning behind a prediction is essential, this lack of openness can be troublesome. Techniques in explainable artificial intelligence (XAI), including saliency maps, feature attribution methods, and surrogate models that replicate the behaviour of complicated networks using interpretable models, have evolved out of attempts to solve this problem.

The requirement for large volumes of labelled data—which can be costly and time-consuming to gather—is another major challenge. Transfer learning, self-supervised learning, and semi-supervised learning have shown promise as means of lessening this reliance. These techniques respectively use unlabelled data, learn from the structure of the data itself, or transfer knowledge from one task to another. Pre-trained models on big datasets, for example, can be finely tweaked on smaller, task-specific datasets, hence greatly lowering the demand for vast labelled samples. In fields with restricted data availability, this has especially proven helpful since it allows deep learning to be implemented in more specialized and delicate uses.

Furthermore, raising questions regarding energy usage and environmental effects is the growing scale and complexity of deep learning models. Large-scale models' training calls for significant computational resources, which fuels great carbon emissions and energy consumption. Growing interest in model efficiency brought about by this has spurred study in methods such as model pruning, quantization, knowledge distillation, and effective designs, including MobileNets and EfficientNet. More suited for deployment on edge devices and in resource-limited situations, these developments seek to lower the computing footprint of deep learning models without compromising performance.

Furthermore, heavily influencing the development and application of deep learning systems are ethical issues. Training data bias might result in biased predictions, therefore supporting social inequities and extending negative preconceptions. Research and policy-making in artificial intelligence systems now revolve mostly around guaranteeing justice, responsibility, and openness in them. This covers attempts to create principles for ethical AI development, build fairness-aware learning algorithms, and audit models for prejudice. Responsible use of deep learning calls for not only technological answers but also multidisciplinary cooperation among computer scientists, ethicists, legal experts, and representatives from impacted populations.

Apart from ethical and technical difficulties, growing research orientations and multidisciplinary integration are influencing the direction of deep learning going forward. Seeking to create models that not only perform well but also throw insight into how biological intelligence operates, one fascinating field is the intersection of deep learning with neuroscience, cognitive science, and psychology. Aiming to mix the logical rigor of symbolic artificial intelligence with the statistical powers of deep learning, another exciting area is the integration of symbolic reasoning with neural networks. This hybrid method seeks to create systems with generalizing across domains, data-driven capability, reasoning, planning, and capacity.

Deep learning and neural networks have effects well beyond scholarly study into people's daily lives all around. From tailored suggestions on streaming platforms to real-time language translating, from medical diagnostics to smart assistants, these technologies have transformed our interactions with knowledge, tools, and each other. Deep learning is being used by companies in everything from transportation and agriculture to healthcare and finance to improve operations, boost decision-making, and generate fresh value. As technology develops, its impact is probably going to grow even more, inspiring change and invention in many spheres of life.

A worldwide community of learners and innovators has been created in great part by educational projects and free access to deep learning tools. Online classes, tutorials, open-source tools, and community forums have made it feasible for people from all backgrounds to interact with deep learning, try real-world data, and help the field. More inclusive and varied engagement in AI development is made possible by this democratization of knowledge, which has sped up the pace of discovery and reduced the entrance obstacles.

Ultimately, the development of artificial intelligence, neural networks, and deep learning marks a historic turn. These technologies have attained hitherto unheard-of performance in a wide range of activities, often competing with or surpassing human capacities by allowing robots to develop sophisticated representations from data. Their transforming power, pragmatic efficiency, and conceptual grace define the direction of intelligent systems going forward. Even if interpretability, data needs, computational efficiency, and ethical responsibility still present difficulties, continuous research and cooperation help to push the envelope of what is feasible. Looking ahead, neural networks and deep learning will surely stay at the vanguard of AI innovation, guiding development toward more capable, responsible, and human-centred technology.

Clustering, Dimensionality Reduction, and Anomaly Detection - Explore unsupervised learning techniques and their uses in real-world scenarios

Three potent methods in the field of artificial intelligence and machine learning—clustering, dimensionality reduction, and anomaly detection—each have special purposes in revealing latent patterns, streamlining difficult data, and spotting rare or odd events. These techniques are especially well-known in unsupervised learning, in which case the system must find structure in the incoming data on its own rather than having labelled data. Common in real-world applications, they provide a strong toolbox together for making sense of big, high-dimensional, often chaotic information. Every technique tackles a distinct facet of data interpretation, and their combined application has been crucial in many disciplines, like fraud detection, bioinformatics, customer segmentation, and cybersecurity.

Without depending on predetermined labels, clustering is a method used to group comparable data points together depending on intrinsic traits or patterns in the data. Clustering aims to divide a dataset into groups whereby data points inside one cluster are more comparable to one another than in those in other clusters. Depending on the type of data and the clustering method applied, one can describe this idea of similarity in several ways. Often the first stage in exploratory data analysis, clustering offers an understanding of the inherent structure of data. K-means is one of the most well-known clustering techniques since it seeks to minimize variance inside each of the k clusters, therefore separating the data. It starts by randomly initializing k centroids and then repeatedly refines them by allocating each data point to the closest centroid and thereby updating the centroids depending on the mean of the allocated points. Simple and computationally efficient, k-means make the assumption that clusters are spherical and evenly sized—which might not always be suitable for real-world data. Certain of these restrictions are addressed by more complex algorithms, including DBSCAN and hierarchical clustering. Either by successively merging or separating clusters depending on distance criteria, hierarchical clustering creates a tree of clusters. Effective at finding clusters of arbitrary shape and spotting outliers as noise, Density-Based Spatial Clustering of Applications with Noise, or DBSCAN, finds clusters as areas of high density separated by areas of low density.

Conversely, dimensionality reduction is focused on minimizing the number of features or variables in a dataset such that as much of the original information as feasible is maintained. Often called the "curse of dimensionality, high-dimensional data can cause overfitting, processing complexity, and trouble with visualization and interpretation. By converting data into a lower-dimensional space and so enabling more effective processing and clearer insights, dimensionality reduction helps to solve these problems. One often used linear technique for dimensionality reduction is principal component analysis (PCA). PCA projects the data onto the directions—that is, the primary components—along which the data fluctuates the most. This produces a fresh collection of uncorrelated features capturing the most important data variance. Although PCA is interpretable and efficient, it makes linear assumptions and could not work effectively if the data's underlying structure is nonlinear. Developed for such situations are nonlinear dimensionality reduction methods, including Uniform Manifold Approximation and Projection (UMAP) and t-Distributed Stochastic Neighbour Embedding (t-SNE). These techniques are especially well-liked for viewing high-dimensional data since they expose intricate features like manifolds and clusters that linear techniques would overlook. Though they can misrepresent distances and are sensitive to parameter settings, they are sometimes employed for visualization rather than downstream machine learning chores.

Anomaly detection—also referred to as outlier detection—focuses on spotting rare or unexpected observations that differ greatly from the norm. These anomalies could point to medical issues, equipment breakdowns, network attacks, or fraudulent transactions—all of which are important events. Because of their rare incidence and perhaps great diversity in what defines an anomaly, detecting anomalies is difficult. Conventional anomaly detection systems depend on statistical approaches assuming a given data distribution and flag points outside of a confidence interval. These techniques, meantime, may find difficulty with complex or high-dimensional data sets. More flexible methods are provided by machine learning-based anomaly-detecting systems. One such technique that randomly chooses a characteristic and subsequently a split value between the maximum and minimum values of that feature isolates anomalies. This approach's reasoning is that since anomalies are few and unique, they are easier to separate. Other methods include autoencoders—neural networks taught to rebuild their input—and One-Class SVM, which learns a decision boundary spanning most of the data and treats everything beyond that boundary as an anomaly. Usually reconstructing regular instances successfully when trained on normal data, an autoencoder performs badly on anomalies and allows their detection depending on reconstruction error.

Although every one of these methods—clustering, dimensionality reduction, and anomaly detection—can be applied alone—they usually perform best when combined. For high-dimensional data, for example, dimensionality reduction can simplify the data structure, eliminate noise, and raise cluster separability before performing clustering. Analogous to this, clustering can help spot anomalies by pointing out points either far from the cluster centres' or outside of any cluster. By concentrating on the most useful features of the data, dimensionality reduction methods can help improve anomaly detection, hence strengthening the signal-to-noise ratio. By means of this interaction between methodologies, data scientists and machine learning practitioners can tackle challenging problems more holistically and derive useful insights otherwise latent in raw data.

Practically speaking, these methods have proved rather helpful in a variety of fields. Clustering is widely used in marketing to group consumers according to purchase behaviour, therefore enabling companies to customize their plans and raise customer happiness. Dimensionality reduction is used in healthcare to simplify genomic data such that hundreds of features per sample make sense in terms of genetic expressions connected to disease. A pillar of fraud detection systems in finance, anomaly detection finds odd trends in transaction data that can indicate illegal behaviour. Predictive maintenance systems in manufacturing use clustering and anomaly detection to find equipment likely to break, therefore allowing timely intervention and lowering downtime. In cybersecurity, the capacity to spot abnormalities in network traffic can notify managers of possible breaches or incursions, usually before major damage is done.

Another important factor is the interpretability of the produced outcomes by these methods. After dimensionality reduction, clustering findings are commonly shown visually on scatter plots, with each cluster allocated a different colour. These representations support stakeholders in comprehending the fundamental data structure and hence validate the success of the clustering technique. Analogous to this, dimensionality reduction methods like as PCA allow one to investigate the contribution of every original feature to the main components, therefore revealing the features causing variation. In anomaly detection, trust and actionability depend on knowing why a certain instance was identified as an abnormality. Visualization tools and feature importance measures help to understand model results and enable data scientists and domain experts to collaboration.

These methods have several limits, notwithstanding their advantages. Although the number of clusters and initial conditions may not always be known in advance, clustering techniques can be sensitive to both. Sometimes, dimensionality reduction techniques lose crucial information, particularly in cases when the data variance is not a suitable indicator of importance. Particularly with noisy data or when the notion of normal behaviour is dubious, anomaly detection can produce false positives or false negatives. Dealing with these difficulties sometimes calls for a thorough awareness of the data, domain knowledge, and iterative experimentation to optimize models and parameters. Moreover, scalable implementations and distributed computing frameworks become ever more crucial to apply these techniques effectively as datasets get in size and complexity.

These techniques become much more important in the big data age. Modern digital systems produce so much data and variation that hand analysis is impossible. Navigating the data tsunami becomes mostly dependent on automated approaches for structure discovery, simplicity reduction, and identification of important outliers. Advances in processing power, together with the development of efficient libraries and cloud-based services, have made it feasible to apply these approaches at scale, therefore enabling companies to generate value from data that would have otherwise been unreachable.

Additionally, under active study are the theoretical foundations of clustering, dimensionality reduction, and anomaly detection. New algorithms and frameworks are under development, either introducing whole new paradigms or combining the best features of current approaches. Often enhancing results in complex datasets, deep learning-based clustering methods, for instance, use neural networks to develop feature representations fit for clustering. For dimensionality reduction and anomaly detection, also under investigation are deep generative models including Generative Adversarial Networks (GANs) and Variational Autoencoders (VAEs). These models give fresh opportunities for data synthesis, denoising, and outlier analysis by learning a compressed representation of the data and being able to create new instances that reflect the original data.

The integration of these methods into end-to-end machine learning pipelines presents still another fascinating direction. Modern artificial intelligence systems generally include dimensionality reduction, anomaly detection, or clustering instead of employing them alone as preprocessing, feature engineering, or monitoring components. Before training a predictive model, for example, dimensionality reduction can be used to lower overfitting and increase performance. In semi-supervised learning systems, clustering can define classes or regions. Anomaly detection functions as a warning system for human intervention or retraining and tracks live systems for unanticipated behaviour.

The relevance of knowing and using clustering, dimensionality reduction, and anomaly detection changes as artificial intelligence develops. These methods offer fundamental capabilities supporting more sophisticated models and systems. For every artificial intelligence practitioner, their interpretability, adaptability, and application across several fields are indispensable instruments. These approaches provide strong solutions based on statistical and computational ideas, whether the objective is to group like consumers, streamline complicated genetic profiles, or detect fraudulent transactions before they get more serious.

All things considered, the machine learning toolkit consists of absolutely essential components: clustering, dimensionality reduction, and anomaly detection. They help to find trends, simplify difficult material, and spot anomalies that would point to risk or opportunity. Although every method has difficulties, the continuous development of tools, algorithms, and theoretical frameworks keeps improving their relevance and efficiency. Mastery of these techniques and knowledge of their interactions will enable practitioners to uncover deeper insights, create more dependable systems, and help to responsibly and creatively advance artificial intelligence in modern society.

CHAPTER V

AI in Action

Natural Language Processing (NLP) - Explore how AI understands and generates human language, including chatbots and translation

Often known as NLP, natural language processing is a potent and transforming field of artificial intelligence with an eye on the interactions between computers and human language. It is focused on allowing machines to produce human language in a way that is both significant and practical by reading, interpreting, understanding, and generating. Fundamentally, NLP closes the distance between the ordered, logical world of machines and the unstructured, frequently uncertain character of human discourse. Language is intrinsically complicated; it is shaped by environment, culture, and personal experience. NLP has to consider all these aspects if we are to reach successful communication between humans and machines. With uses ranging from virtual assistants and machine translation to sentiment analysis, content summarizing, and beyond, NLP is clearly important in today's technology scene. NLP is a critical enabler of intelligent, human-like communication as people engage with technology utilizing speech and text more and more.

The history of NLP is closely entwined with the general evolution of artificial intelligence. Early initiatives in the 1950s and 1960s sprang from rule-based systems, in which computers were programmed using large sets of grammatical and syntactic rules intended to process and translate languages. But soon, it became clear that language was too complex to be fully expressed by set guidelines. With researchers using probabilistic models that discovered patterns from the vast corpus of text, the development of statistical approaches in the 1990s signalled a dramatic change. More complex and accurate NLP systems were made possible by this data-driven approach, which also allowed for more flexibility and adaptation. NLP capabilities have advanced exponentially with the advent of machine learning—and, more recently, deep learning. Driven by big neural networks and trained on vast amounts of data, today's systems can create cohesive sections, respond to challenging queries, and even show a basic awareness of context and emotion.

Tokenizing—the process of dissecting text into smaller bits such as words, sub words, or characters—is one of the fundamental chores in natural language processing. Since it converts unprocessable text into a format algorithm can operate with, this stage is essential for more investigation and processing. Other preprocessing techniques, such as stemming and lemmatization, are sometimes used following tokenization to help words be reduced to their base or root forms. These methods increase model generalization and aid in lowering language variation. Another crucial component of natural language processing, part-of-speech tagging, assigns grammatical categories—such as nouns, verbs, adjectives, and so forth—to words. Particularly in parsing and machine translation, this material is quite helpful for grasping phrase structure and meaning.

Another important chore in natural language processing (NLP) is called entity recognition (NER), which involves matching proper nouns in text into specified categories, including individuals, companies, places, dates, and numerical expressions. Information extraction depends much on NER, which helps systems to extract ordered knowledge from unstructured text. In a news item on a business merger, for instance, an NLP system with NER capabilities may find the names of the organizations engaged, the merger date, and any pertinent financial data. NER helps to clarify stories and relationships in the text by means of co-reference resolution—which marks when many expressions relate to the same entity—so fostering a better knowledge of them.

A common usage of natural language processing (NLP), sentiment analysis seeks to identify the subjective opinion or emotional tone conveyed in a work of text. Sentiment analysis enables companies to evaluate public opinion and react accordingly, whether they are reviewing products, social media posts, customer comments, or elsewhere. Given the intricacies of language—including sarcasm, idioms, and context-dependent meanings—this work can be especially difficult. Modern NLP systems leverage contextual word embeddings and attention mechanisms to attain state-of-the-art performance in sentiment classification using advanced techniques like transformer-based models like BERT and GPT.

Another highly important field of NLP is machine translation, which lets text or speech from one language automatically be translated into another. Early rule-based systems sometimes produced embarrassing translations and had limited vocabulary. Though they still battled with long-range dependencies and unusual word combinations, statistical techniques improved fluency.

The discipline was transformed when neural machine translation—especially with regard to sequence-to-sequence models with attention mechanisms—became available. These models capture idioms and cultural quirks, therefore enabling translations that are not only grammatically accurate but also contextually suitable. Using these technologies, services like Google Translate and DeepL offer real-time, high-quality translations across dozens of languages, therefore overcoming linguistic barriers on a worldwide basis.

Another interesting NLP chore is text summarizing, which is compiling a cogent and succinct overview of a more extensive body of work. Summarizing can be either abstractive—where the algorithm creates new sentences with the necessary meaning of the input—or extractive, in which case important sentences or phrases from the original text are chosen. Particularly difficult is abstractive summarizing since it calls for both a thorough knowledge of the material and the capacity for the synthesis of fresh ideas. Pre-trained language models and deep learning advances have greatly improved the quality of automated summaries, hence increasing their usability and information value.

Among the most engaging and user-facing NLP applications are conversational agents and question answering systems. Often, by accessing pertinent information from a database or corpus, question answering systems are meant to give users accurate and succinct responses to their questions. Particularly difficult and a standard for NLP research is open-domain question answering, whereby the system must respond to questions without any predetermined context. Combining several NLP features—including speech recognition, intent categorization, and dialogue management—chatbots and virtual assistants like Siri, Alexa, and Google Assistant help users have natural and significant discussions. These systems have to not only grasp user input but also keep context between turns, control uncertainty, and offer relevant and useful answers.

A basic feature of natural language processing, language modelling underlies many of the more sophisticated uses noted above. A language model captures the chance of one word following another by giving sequences of word probabilities. Conventional models, including n-grams, suffered from sparsity problems and employed fixed-length settings. Maintaining hidden states over sequences, recurrent neural networks (RNNs), and subsequently, Long Short-Term Memory (LSTM) networks addressed these problems by allowing the modelling of longer contexts. The true innovation, though, came with the creation of transformer architectures, which included self-attention systems enabling models to evaluate the relative value of various words in a sequence. Modern NLP models such as BERT (Bidirectional Encoder Representations from Transformers) and GPT (Generative Pre-trained Transformer), which have shown amazing performance over a broad spectrum of jobs, are based on transformers.

Pre-trained language models have transformed the field of natural language processing quite substantially. Training on a large corpus of text helps these models develop a general knowledge of language that can be modified for particular tasks with quite limited labelled input. By democratizing access to strong NLP skills, this transfer learning method has let academics and developers create complex systems without using vast computational resources or big datasets. For jobs including sentiment analysis, question answering, and text classification—where BERT has been optimized—she has produced state-of-the-art results in each. With their autoregressive character, GPT models shine in text generation, narrative, and creative writing; their outputs are sometimes exactly like those created by humans.

NLP still suffers several difficulties even with these developments. Ambiguity is one of the most recurring problems since, depending on context, one word or statement could have several connotations. For instance, the word "bank" could refer to a side of a river or a financial organization; so, knowing the right meaning depends on knowing the surrounding words and the more general conversation. Dealing with such issues calls for models that not only absorb text but also encode common sense information and world wisdom. Another difficulty is bias, which model outputs can unintentionally reflect from training data. Ethical questions of fairness, openness, and responsibility in NLP systems arise from language models learned on online text picking up and spreading unpleasant content or stereotypes.

Another frontier is multilingual natural language processing, which seeks to create models that perform well across several languages—especially ones with low resources. Although English boasts a lot of labelled data and computational tools, many languages lack both. This difference results in a mismatch in NLP technology performance and accessibility. To solve this problem, cross-lingual models and transfer learning techniques are under investigation so that knowledge acquired in high-resource languages may be used in low-resource ones. Large-scale translations and multilingual BERT versions help to create a more inclusive and fair future for NLP.

From real-time multilingual communication and tailored tutoring systems to sympathetic AI companions and clever writing assistance, NLP has fascinating opportunities ahead. Making models more efficient, interpretable, and consistent with human values is also becoming more important as they keep getting bigger and more capable. Distillation, trimming, and quantization are among the methods meant to lower the computational footprint of big models, thereby increasing their availability and sustainability. Explainable NLP aims to make model decisions clear so that consumers may better know why a certain output was produced. Furthermore, in development are models for matching NLP systems with ethical standards and human purposes to guarantee the responsible application of these technologies.

At the junction of linguistics, computer science, and artificial intelligence, Natural Language Processing finally shows a dynamic and fast developing area. It enables machines to comprehend and engage with human language in ways once the purview of science fiction. From basic keyword searches to sophisticated dialogue systems, natural language processing influences almost every facet of our digital existence. Driven by improvements in algorithms, processing capability, and the availability of big datasets, the path from rule-based systems to transformer-based language models has been marked by major discoveries. Still, the trip is not quite finished. The possibilities for invention remain great as practitioners and researchers keep stretching the bounds of what NLP can accomplish. NLP is evidence of the transforming potential of artificial intelligence in comprehending and using the richness of human language, whether it be enabling more inclusive communication, improving education and accessibility, or generating new forms of artistic expression.

Computer Vision - Explain how machines "see" and interpret visual data, from facial recognition to self-driving cars

Within artificial intelligence, computer vision is a fascinating and fast developing field with an emphasis on helping robots to comprehend and grasp the visual environment. Fundamentally, computer vision aims to imitate the human capacity for image and video perception, recognition, and sense of direction. Using sophisticated algorithms, deep learning methods, and enormous volumes of visual data, this multifarious field teaches computers to derive meaningful information from the pixels they view. Computer vision is first in bridging the gap between visual perception and computational intelligence whether it be object recognition in images, face identification, motion detection, or scene interpretation in a video feed. The quest for this competence has resulted in major innovations in many sectors, including healthcare, automotive, security, agriculture, retail, and more, so changing our interaction with and advantage from technology.

Computer vision started in the early days of artificial intelligence when scientists started to consider if machines might be made to see. Early tests were modest, utilizing handcrafted filters and rule-based systems to detect edges or recognize basic shapes. During these first years, a lack of processing capability and the intricacy of visual input hindered development. However, the expansion of digital images, along with the evolution of more potent CPUs and the arrival of machine learning, set the stage for major breakthroughs. Deep learning and convolutional neural networks (CNNs) changed the discipline dramatically and enabled amazing accuracy in formerly thought impossible jobs. These developments let computers understand hierarchical patterns in visual input, thereby automatically identifying characteristics required for tasks, including segmentation, image classification, and object detection.

One of the fundamental challenges in computer vision is picture classification, in which case the objective is to classify an entire image depending on its content. Because of the great diversity in lighting, orientation, background, and object appearance, this chore—which seems straightforward for humans—is quite difficult for machines. Early methods of image classification followed machine learning techniques like support vector machines after mostly depending on manual feature extraction, such as edge detection and texture or colour histograms. But when CNNs emerged, picture classification performance experienced a notable drop. By means of a sequence of convolutional layers, pooling procedures, and nonlinear activations, CNNs automatically learn to recognize pertinent features from raw pixel input. CNNs' performance in large-scale picture classification tasks such as ImageNet, where models trained from millions of labelled images, marked a turning point in the field and inspired the broad acceptance of deep learning approaches in computer vision.

Object detection goes beyond categorization to include not just object recognition but also localizing bounding boxes around each occurrence in an image. Applications like autonomous driving, where a car must instantly identify pedestrians, other automobiles, traffic signals, and hazards, depend on this work. Popular object identification systems such as Faster R-CNN, SSD (Single Shot Multibox Detector), and YOLO (You Only Look Once) have stretched the envelope of both speed and accuracy. These models permit effective real-time detection by combining localization and classification under a single architecture. Modern computer vision systems now mostly rely on object detection to let robots analyze intricate visual environments and act accordingly depending on what they sense.

Image segmentation assigns a class label to every pixel in an image, therefore separating the image into areas of interest and so transcending visual knowledge. Semantic segmentation—which labels pixels of the same class—and instance segmentation—which distinguishes between distinct objects of the same class—are two main forms of segmentation. Particularly in fields like medical imaging, where exact delineation of anatomical features can help in diagnosis and treatment planning, techniques including

U-Net, Mask R-CNN, and DeepLab have proven vital in enhancing segmentation accuracy. Applications such as augmented reality, robotics, and video surveillance also depend on image segmentation since interaction and navigation depend on knowledge of the spatial arrangement of a scene.

Facial recognition—the ability of computer vision to identify or validate people depending on facial characteristics—is still another strong capacity of it. Security systems, cell phones, and even social media sites now feature this technology extensively. To create a digital signature that can be matched against a database, facial recognition algorithms examine individual patterns in a person's face—such as the distance between the eyes, the form of the nose, and the contour of the jawline. Although facial recognition presents improved security and convenience, it has also generated major privacy, prejudice, and surveillance issues. Problems include racial and gender prejudice in recognition accuracy have led to calls for more ethical development methods in the application of such systems and more control.

Still, another exciting field in computer vision is motion analysis and video interpretation. These chores track objects, evaluate sequences of photos across time to find movement, and grasp activities or behaviours. Applications span gesture detection and sports analytics to traffic surveillance and human activity recognition. Commonly used in this setting are optical flow algorithms—which evaluate object apparent motion in a video—and recurrent neural networks—which describe temporal interdependence. More recently, to capture spatiotemporal patterns, 3D convolutional networks, and transformer-based models have been presented, so enhancing the knowledge of complicated motion and interactions inside video content.

Beyond flat, two-dimensional vision, 3D vision—that which allows robots to grasp depth and spatial relationships—expansion of computer vision. Technologies such as stereo vision, LiDAR (Light Detection and Ranging), and structured light let systems see the world in three dimensions, therefore enabling applications in autonomous cars, robotics, and augmented reality. For self-driving automobiles, for example, precise assessment of the distance and speed of surrounding objects depends on 3D perception. In industrial robotics, 3D vision similarly lets robots precisely move goods in challenging surroundings. Combining 2D image data with depth information helps to provide a richer, more complex knowledge of scenes, therefore enabling machines to interact with the world in a more human-like manner.

Particularly via Generative Adversarial Networks (GANs), generative modelling is among the most fascinating developments in computer vision. Two neural networks—a generator and a discriminator—that fight in a zero-sum game—where the generator generates synthetic images and the discriminator seeks to differentiate them from actual ones—make GANs. Highly realistic images created by this adversarial training method find use in art, design, data augmentation, and even medical research. Where the content of one image is displayed in the manner of another, GANs have also made possible methods, including image-to-image translation, super-resolution, and stylistic transfer. These technologies create ethical questions about the production of deepfakes and the manipulation of visual media, even as they provide fresh creative opportunities.

In computer vision, pre-trained models and transfer learning have become indispensable instruments since they let practitioners apply the information gained from big datasets to new, smaller problems with limited data. Pre-trained on ImageNet, models such as ResNet, VGG, and EfficientNet provide strong foundations for many different kinds of uses. Through domain-specific data fine-tuning of these models, developers can attain great performance with low computational resources and training times. This method has democratized access to state-of-the-art computer vision technology, allowing companies with minimal resources to create advanced visual systems as well as researchers.

Its promise is enhanced even more by the combination of computer vision with other artificial intelligence fields. Combining natural language processing with medical imaging helps to create intelligent diagnostic systems in healthcare that can examine scans and produce thorough reports. By means of user preferences and behaviour analysis, vision-based systems coupled with recommendation engines can provide tailored shopping experiences in retail. Using computer vision, drones fitted for agriculture can track crop health and maximize resource use. By spotting flaws in manufacturing lines, vision systems guarantee quality control. These diverse uses underline the adaptability and transforming ability of computer vision in many fields.

Computer vision has continuous difficulties, even with its amazing successes. Generalization—the capacity of models to operate well on unseen data—is one of the basic challenges. Models trained on particular datasets may find difficulty with different lighting conditions, backdrops, or item variances since visual environments are naturally changing. Solving this problem calls for more solid training plans, including self-supervised learning, domain adaptation, and data augmentation. Explainability is another difficulty since deep learning models may act as black boxes, and it is hard to know how judgments are taken. Building trust and guaranteeing responsibility depend on developing interpretable vision systems that reveal insights into their reasoning processes.

Another important issue with visual datasets is bias since imbalances in the training data could produce unfair or erroneous results. For instance, facial recognition systems taught mostly on some groups may fail on others, therefore extending socioeconomic inequities. Creating fair vision systems depends on both strict evaluation across demographic groups and diversity and representativeness in datasets. Moreover, ethical issues have to direct the application of computer vision, especially in law enforcement, surveillance, and other sensitive environments where abuse might have grave results.

Many developing developments will help to define computer vision's direction going forward. One is the shift toward more lightweight and economical models like smartphones, drones, and IoT sensors that can run on edge devices with low processing capacity. This change makes real-time vision applications possible in distributed systems free from depending on cloud architecture. Another tendency is the convergence of vision and language, best shown by models like CLIP and DALL·E, who grasp visuals in the framework of natural language prompts. Simpler human-computer interactions are made possible by these models, which also release fresh possibilities in cross-modally comprehension and creativity.

Computer vision is probably going to become more and more woven into the fabric of daily life as it develops, impacting our job, education, communication, and leisure time activities. From improving access for those with vision problems to allowing immersive virtual experiences, the opportunities are many and different. Harnessing the full potential of computer vision while addressing related dangers and constraints will depend on ongoing research combined with responsible development and deployment techniques. In the end, computer vision marks not only a technical triumph but also a significant increase in the possibilities for robots to interact with their surroundings. It turns pixels into knowledge, images into insight, and in doing so helps us to realize the promise of really intelligent systems able to see, interpret, and react to the richness of the visual environment.

Predictive Analytics and Recommender Systems - Dive into systems that anticipate user behaviour and suggest content, products, or actions

Two of the most powerful and often used applications of artificial intelligence are predictive analytics and recommender systems, which transform raw data into foresight and personalization, therefore impacting many sectors. These technologies are based on the capacity to identify trends in real-time and historical data and then use them to project future preferences or events. In a world going more and more data-driven, the capacity to predict results and meet personal demands has evolved from a competitive edge into an expectation. Originating in statistical modelling and machine learning, predictive analytics aims to project results, including consumer behaviour, market trends, or operational hazards. Conversely, recommender systems promote goods, services, or information based on prior behaviour and inferred preferences using similar methods. Together, they create a vital link between data collecting and decision-making, so interactions with digital systems become more smart, responsive, and pertinent.

Predictive analytics is fundamentally based on its capacity to turn past data into useful insights. Fundamentally, this process includes data-based relationship identification, model creation that catches these trends, and application of those models to estimate future behaviour or results. These models range in complexity from ensemble approaches and neural networks to as straightforward as linear regression equations. Predictive analytics is used by companies to answer many kinds of questions: Which clients are probably going to leave? Next quarter, what will demand look like? In what ways might a pricing change affect sale? These data-based forecasts help companies go from reactive to proactive decision-making. Trained on labelled data, including both input variables and the outcomes of interest, predictive models are trained, and the model can be used to forecast new, unprocessed data. The quality of the data, the fit of the modelling method, and the significance of the chosen characteristics for training determine the accuracy of these forecasts.

Predictive analytics is now absolutely essential in the business world for financial forecasting, marketing optimization, fraud detection, and customer relationship management. Credit card issuers, for example, track transaction data in real time to identify possibly fraudulent behaviour depending on deviations from accepted trends. In the same vein, insurance companies evaluate risk and decide policy prices using predictive algorithms. Predictive analytics helps retailers focus promotions on the most sensitive consumer groups, control inventory, and project sales. These methods are used in the healthcare sector to evaluate disease risk, forecast patient readmissions, and customize therapy programs. Predictive analytics is used even by sports teams to maximize player performance and strategy. As access to vast, varied datasets and computational capability grows, the range of applications keeps widening.

Remarkably changing user interaction with digital content, recommender systems parallel the development of predictive analytics. From movie recommendations on streaming platforms to product recommendations on e-commerce sites, these systems customize experiences to fit specific consumers, hence improving pleasure and involvement. Usually falling into three primary groups, recommender systems are content-based filtering, hybrid techniques, and collaborative filtering. Content-based filtering matches users to objects with like qualities based on their attributes and user preferences. Unlike collaborative filtering, which finds trends among users and products based on past interactions, presuming individuals who loved similar things in the past will continue to do so, will Combining aspects of both helps hybrid systems to overcome their individual constraints and raise recommendation quality.

The fast expansion of digital content and the need to sort through enormous volumes of data help considerably in the general adoption of recommender systems. Users would suffer to locate pertinent objects in oceans of data without these systems. To suggest movies and series according to a user's viewing history, ratings, and behaviour of like users, for instance, Netflix uses advanced recommender algorithms based on browsing past, purchases, and user similarities, and Amazon suggests items. Using listening patterns and combining them with other users' musical choices, Spotify creates customized playlists. By improving user retention, raising sales, and encouraging more thorough platform interaction, these systems not only improve user pleasure but also generate corporate results.

The availability and quality of user data determine the degree of recommender system efficacy. Often reflecting user preferences more precisely than explicit data like ratings or reviews, implicit data include clicks, views, and purchase history but gathering and analysing this information begs serious privacy and ethical questions. The development of recommender systems depends mostly on finding a compromise between privacy and customization. Maintaining trust and compliance with data protection rules depends critically on openness in how suggestions are produced, giving consumers a choice over their data, and protecting private information.

Though their goals and applications differ, predictive analytics and recommender systems depend on comparable machine learning approaches and data science concepts. Often, for operational or strategic decision-making, predictive analytics centres on anticipating particular results. Although they are predictive as well, recommender systems stress user interaction and personalization. Notwithstanding these differences, the two fields find more and more convergence in application. A marketing platform might, for example, use predictive models to identify which consumers are likely to respond to a campaign and then apply a recommender system to customize the material of that campaign. Predictive analytics can help e-commerce identify high-value consumers; meanwhile, recommender systems customize shopping experiences to enhance conversion and loyalty.

Usually following a disciplined workflow, these systems begin with data collecting and preprocessing. Many times, noisy, incomplete, or inconsistent, raw data needs cleaning, normalizing, and transformation to be useable. Model performance depends critically on feature engineering—the process of choosing and building meaningful variables. This can mean encoding user demographics, item properties, or interaction histories for recommender systems. Features in predictive models could be aggregate statistics, categorical markers, or time series patterns. The data is separated into training and testing sets once ready to assess generalizability and model correctness.

A crucial phase, depending on the type of the problem, data properties, and performance criteria, is model selection. While more complicated models like gradient boosting machines or deep neural networks give greater accuracy at the sacrifice of transparency, simpler models like decision trees or logistic regression offer interpretability and ease of deployment. Matrix factorization methods, including singular value decomposition (SVD), have shown good success in recommender systems for capturing latent user-item interactions. Autoencoders and recurrent neural networks, among other deep learning models, improve the ability of recommender systems to replicate complicated, nonlinear relationships and temporal dynamics.

Context influences the evaluation criteria. Metrics including accuracy, precision, recall, F1 score, and area under the ROC curve are typical in predictive analytics. Precision at k, recall at k, mean average precision, and normalized discounted cumulative gain are applied in recommender systems to evaluate how closely the recommendations fit user preferences. Online testing techniques, including A/B testing and multivariate testing, help to augment offline evaluation grounded on historical data by measuring real-world performance and user effect.

Another key issue in all fields is scalability, particularly for web-based solutions. Large datasets and real-time forecasts demand techniques, including distributed computing, parallel processing, and the application of effective data structures. Big data systems include Apache Spark and Hadoop, as well as cloud computing platforms that offer the foundation required to create and implement scalable predictive and recommender systems. Mechanisms for model retraining and continual learning guarantee that systems change with changing user behaviour and outside environment, hence preserving relevance and accuracy over time.

Predictive analytics and recommender systems' design and implementation now give ethical issues rising relevance. Personal data use has to be legitimate, open, and consistent with user expectations. In data or algorithms, bias could provide unjust results, such as biased credit scoring or the reinforcement of societal prejudices in recommendations. Dealing with these problems calls for a dedication to inclusiveness in artificial intelligence development, justice, and responsibility. Workflows include explainability tools, fairness-aware learning, and bias mitigating strategies to find and fix troublesome trends.

Particularly explainability is becoming more and more important as users ask to know how artificial intelligence systems decide. Particularly in high-stakes fields like banking and healthcare, model interpretability is absolutely vital in predictive analytics for regulatory compliance and stakeholder confidence. Methods such as LIME (Local Interpretable Model-agnostic Explanations) and SHAP (Shapley Additive Explanations) offer an understanding of feature importance and model behaviour. Explainable recommendations let users understand why particular things are recommended, thereby promoting openness and trust in the system and so increasing user satisfaction in recommender systems.

Advancements in artificial intelligence, the availability of richer data sources, and changing user expectations will help to influence predictive analytics and recommender systems going forward. Integration of contextual awareness—that of location, time, and emotional state—will improve the timeliness and relevancy of predictions and suggestions. An area of growing study is a cross-domain recommendation, in which ideas from one domain—e.g., music tastes—inform recommendations in another—e.g., books or travel. Combining text, graphics, audio, and behavioural data in multi-modal systems provides a more complete picture of user preferences and helps to enable more advanced personalizing.

Future systems will thus have to give justice, openness, and user control a top priority, as the growing focus on responsible artificial intelligence clearly indicates. New norms for responsibility and ethics in artificial intelligence are being established by legislative frameworks such as GDPR and the European Union's AI Act. From data collecting and model training to deployment and monitoring, organizations will have to include ethical issues at every level of system architecture. This change offers not only a legal need but also a chance to create better user-centric, trustworthy, inclusive platforms.

In the end, recommender systems and predictive analytics show how practically artificial intelligence can derive meaning from data and improve human decision-making. They help companies forecast demands, consumers find novel experiences, and society run more effectively and responsively. Their influence will deepen as these technologies develop and affect every part of our digital and physical lives. The difficulty and opportunity lie in using their potential responsibly so that the insights they produce empower people, encourage fair results, and help to create a more intelligent and caring world.

CHAPTER VI

Challenges and Ethics in AI

Bias, Fairness, and Transparency - Examine how bias enters AI systems and the ethical responsibility of developers

In the current era, bias, justice, and openness in artificial intelligence have become fundamental subjects in the evolution, implementation, and control of intelligent systems. From healthcare and education to criminal justice, banking, and employment, as artificial intelligence technologies grow to permeate important spheres of human life—questions about how these systems run and affect individuals have taken the front stage. The discussion of these ideas is not only technical; it covers ethical, legal, and social spheres since artificial intelligence systems make decisions impacting actual people in all spheres. Building systems that represent fair principles and promote trust depends on knowing the foundations of algorithmic bias, the difficulties of applying justice in machine learning, and the need for openness. Without intentional attention to these issues, artificial intelligence may unintentionally reinforce and even exacerbate current societal inequities, therefore causing great damage and systematic injustice.

In artificial intelligence, bias results from several sources, most usually from the data on which machine learning systems are taught. These systems inherit the patterns, hierarchies, and inequalities buried in historical data since they learn from that data. A hiring system trained on resumes from a company that has consistently recruited mostly men, for instance, might learn to favour male candidates and unintentionally discriminate against women. The data reflecting current societal imbalances introduces this kind of bias, not deliberate intent. Data bias can show itself as sample bias, measuring bias, historical bias, and labelling bias, among other things. When the population a model is designed to serve is not sufficiently represented in the dataset used for training, sampling bias results. Measurement bias results from the inability of the selected variables to fairly depict the actual nature of what is being observed for some properties. While labelling bias can develop if human preconceptions or inconsistencies affect the labels provided to training data, historical bias reflects systematic injustices existent in earlier activities.

Through their processing and interpretation of inputs, algorithms themselves can introduce bias even in the absence of biased data. Different demographic groupings can have differences in results enhanced by model architecture, objective functions, and optimization techniques. For instance, a facial recognition system that performs badly for darker-skinned people but well for lighter-skinned people shows algorithmic bias resulting from both data imbalance and model restrictions. This was especially seen in actual systems where facial recognition ability differed greatly depending on gender and colour. Such differences highlight how urgently diversified datasets, inclusive design principles, and strong evaluation techniques—which guarantee fair model performance—are needed.

In artificial intelligence, fairness is a difficult and multifarious notion with no one agreed definition. Practically, depending on the situation and the parties engaged, justice might mean several things. Among the often-used definitions are demographic parity, equal opportunity, equalized odds, and individual fairness. Demographic parity calls for results free of protected characteristics like race or gender. Equal opportunity underlines that, independent of their group membership, those who qualify for a positive outcome should have an equal chance of getting it. Equalized odds go further and call for equal true positive and false positive rates across groups. Individual justice argues for treating like-minded people equally depending on pertinent characteristics. These concepts, however, are sometimes in conflict with one another, and reaching one could mean sacrificing another. This has made people realize that fairness is a value-loaded decision that has to be guided by ethical standards, legal rules, and societal expectations rather than a just quantitative notion.

From data collecting and preprocessing to model selection, training, evaluation, and deployment, implementing justice in machine learning systems calls for a conscious and continuous effort during the AI lifetime. Bias in models can be lessened by reweighting, resampling, adversarial debiasing, and justice-aware learning algorithms. Important instruments for determining whether systems satisfy fairness criteria are fairness-aware benchmarks, impact analyses, and fairness audits. Still, technological answers are insufficient. Furthermore, ingrained in company policies, governance systems, and responsibility structures must be fair. Ensuring that justice reflects a wide range of viewpoints and needs depends on including many stakeholders—

including ethicists, subject specialists, and affected communities.

Another basic component of responsible artificial intelligence development is transparency. Transparency in artificial intelligence refers to the degree to which one may examine and comprehend the internal workings, decision-making process, and data sources of an artificial intelligence system. Public control, confidence, and responsibility all depend on openness. Transparency helps one to evaluate whether artificial intelligence systems are running ethically, making reasonable decisions, or complementing society's values. In opaque systems—often referred to as "black-box" models—stakeholders are left in the dark regarding the rationale behind particular choices. In high-stakes fields like healthcare, banking, and criminal justice—where decisions have major ramifications—this is particularly troublesome.

Transparency-oriented efforts have produced explainable artificial intelligence (XAI) techniques meant to make AI models more understandable. Post-hoc explanations like feature importance scores, counterfactual examples, and surrogate models approximating the behaviour of intricate systems abound in these approaches. For example, SHAP values can show how each feature supported a certain prediction, therefore offering some understanding of the reasoning of the model. Although interpretability usually calls for simplifying difficult models, finding the ideal balance between performance and openness remains a difficult task. When transparency is a top concern, sometimes choosing simpler interpretable models—such as logistic regression or decision trees—may be better even if they are less accurate than more sophisticated options like deep neural networks.

Transparency also entails open records and information on how artificial intelligence systems are developed, tested, and trained. Tools for recording the goals, constraints, and performance of artificial intelligence systems across many settings and populations are model cards, data sheets, and system fact sheets. By allowing outside inspection and informed decision-making by users, developers, and authorities, these documentation processes help to foster responsibility. Transparency also should cover the procedures used in data collecting and labelling, including details on data sources, selection criteria, and labelling techniques. Crucially for the ethical application of artificial intelligence, this all-encompassing approach to transparency promotes an open and responsible culture.

Reinforcing prejudice reduction, justice, and openness in artificial intelligence depends critically on legal and regulatory systems. Guidelines and rules requiring ethical artificial intelligence methods are starting to be developed by governments and international organizations. For high-risk applications, the European Union's AI Act, for example, calls for transparency, human supervision, and robustness and suggests risk-based categories for AI systems. Similar rights over their data are granted under data protection rules including the General Data Protection Regulation (GDPR), which also includes the right to explanation when automated decisions adversely impact them. These legal developments highlight the increasing awareness among society that artificial intelligence has to function inside a framework including public interest, democratic responsibility, and human rights.

By explicitly incorporating values into AI development processes, ethical principles, and human-centred design techniques augment legal frameworks. Respect for autonomy, beneficence, non-maleficence, and fairness direct developers in thinking through the wider consequences of their work. Including ethical impact evaluations, participatory design techniques, and ongoing stakeholder involvement guarantees that artificial intelligence systems benefit all users—especially underprivileged and vulnerable populations. Building a culture of conscientious innovation among developers, data scientists, and decision-makers depends equally on ethics and responsible artificial intelligence education and training.

The junction of prejudice, fairness, and openness also emphasizes the need for diversity in artificial intelligence development teams. Diverse teams are more likely to foresee and solve a greater spectrum of possible negative effects and prejudices, therefore promoting more inclusive technology. Representation of gender, colour, socioeconomic background, and lived experience enhances the points of view included in design and problem-solving techniques. Not just moral requirements, but also pragmatic ways to create more strong and socially sensitive systems are inclusive workplaces and support of fair involvement in AI development.

The larger ecology of AI responsibility depends critically on public understanding and civic involvement. Users have to be equipped with awareness about how artificial intelligence systems impact their lives and with the means to contest unjust or opaque policies. Public consultations, openness reports, and media literacy help to close the technological complexity gap in society's understanding. Advocating rights, exposing injustices, and holding institutions responsible depends much on civil society organizations, scholars, and watchdog groups. The democratization of artificial intelligence governance guarantees that its advantages and drawbacks are distributed fairly instead of concentrated in the hands of a small number of strong organizations.

In the end, tackling prejudice, guaranteeing fairness, and advancing openness in artificial intelligence is an ongoing process of introspection, assessment, and development, not a one-time endeavour. New problems and conundrums will surface as artificial intelligence systems develop and enter ever more spheres of existence. Given the complexity of human society, it is impossible to eradicate all prejudice; rather, the objective is to identify and control it in ways that respect justice, dignity, and human well-being. Integrating ethical foresight, technical rigor, and broad engagement will help us to create artificial intelligence as a tool for good reflecting our best hopes for justice, responsibility, and transparency in a digital society.

Privacy and Surveillance - Discuss the balance between innovation and personal privacy in an AI-driven world

In the debate on artificial intelligence and digital technology, privacy, and monitoring have become significant concerns. The line separating personal autonomy from societal control has grown increasingly hazy in an increasingly linked world where intelligent systems gather, process, and evaluate enormous volumes of data. The capability for surveillance and data collecting has exploded as artificial intelligence finds its way into everything from law enforcement and government infrastructure to smart homes and cell phones. Although these powers can bring great advantages—personalized services, enhanced public safety, and more effective government—they also beg serious concerns about the respect of individual privacy, the possibility of power abuse, and the degradation of basic civil liberties. Deeply complicated and tense, the interaction between artificial intelligence, privacy, and surveillance calls for a delicate balancing act between technical innovation, ethical standards, legal systems, and democratic responsibility.

Modern surveillance is based on data—the raw material running artificial intelligence algorithms. Search histories, location data, social media activity, biometric IDs, or voice recordings—people create enormous digital footprints that are constantly collected by different companies. These databases are not only large but also informative, able to depict in great detail people's lives, activities, tastes, and even ideas. Analysing this information, artificial intelligence algorithms find trends, project future behaviour, and guide decision-making. Although this kind of research can be used to customize ads, enhance user experiences, or find fraud, it also poses major concerns when people are tracked, classified, or rated without their knowledge or permission. The issue is not only that data is being gathered but also that it is being used in an opaque, uncontrolled, maybe discriminating manner.

Many countries now have mass surveillance made possible by artificial intelligence. Often under the pretext of national security, crime prevention, or public health, governments and business enterprises both use advanced technology to track populations. For example, facial recognition technology lets police monitor people in public areas with unheard-of speed and accuracy. By forecasting where crimes would happen based on past crime data, predictive policing systems drive more police presence in some areas and higher monitoring. Proponents contend that these instruments can improve efficiency and safety, while detractors warn that they might cause over-policing, support current prejudices, and destroy public institution confidence. The covert character of monitoring sometimes leaves people uninformed that they are being monitored, therefore affecting freedom of expression, assembly, and association.

Informed permission is one of the fundamental ethical questions driving the privacy argument. Individuals should theoretically be entitled to know when and how their data is being gathered, used, and shared, as well as to be able to opt out should they so want. Practically speaking, though, this goal is hardly fulfilled. Many times, privacy rules are thick, jargon-filled texts most people never read or comprehend. Many times, consent is packaged within terms of service agreements that have to be approved in order to access necessary services, therefore giving users no genuine option. Furthermore, once data is gathered, it can be combined, examined, and sold to third parties in ways that evade user control. Cross-referencing other datasets helps one often re-ident even anonymized data, so it compromises individual privacy.

In authoritarian governments, where official power is centralized, and criticism is typically stifled, the use of artificial intelligence in surveillance raises especially alarming questions. Under such circumstances, artificial intelligence can turn into a tool for political control, allowing governments to track activists, monitor opposition leaders, censor speech, and threaten dissidents. For instance, social credit systems aggregate several data sources to evaluate individuals on their behaviour, therefore influencing their access to public services, employment, and housing as well as their creditworthiness. States have unheard-of control over the lives of their people thanks to the capacity to track populations at scale and with great granularity. These advances cast serious doubt on the fit of artificial intelligence monitoring with democratic norms and undermine the belief that privacy is a universal human right.

The use of artificial intelligence for surveillance needs careful handling, even in democratic countries. Law enforcement authorities could, for example, deploy behavioural analysis tools or facial recognition technologies without enough control, therefore violating both due process and privacy. Surveillance technologies used without public consultation, legal investigations conducted, or openness could lead to a situation whereby strong tools are used with minimal responsibility. To exacerbate the situation, it is not always clear how effective surveillance driven by artificial intelligence is. Those who are unfairly targeted run the risk of suffering negative effects via false positives, erroneous individual identification, or human system manipulation. Many artificial intelligence systems are opaque, so the issue is exacerbated; people impacted by these systems have no means to question decisions or understand how they are reached.

Apart from maintaining secrets, privacy also concerns a person's sovereignty, dignity, and capacity to write their own story. Should one lose control over their personal information, one becomes open to being manipulated, abused, and taken advantage of. For example, targeted advertising has the hidden but enormous power to affect consumer behaviour. Regarding political microtargeting, which uses personal data to provide customized messages meant to change voter emotions, questions have been raised about the integrity of democratic procedures and the danger of manipulation. The concept of surveillance capitalism—business models derived from personal data—has turned privacy into a commodity exchanged for profit devoid of informed permission of people whose life is impacted by it. These dynamic compromises the idea that people should be the last judges of their own knowledge.

In this day of artificial intelligence, one must employ a range of tactics to defend people's privacy. Among these tactics are legislative protections, societal changes, and technological advances. Technologically, homomorphic encryption, differential privacy, and federated learning are all interesting paths that might be followed in methods that safeguard personal privacy. These techniques enable data analysis without revealing specific data points, therefore preserving anonymity and allowing one to get insights without revealing individual facts. Differential privacy, for instance, inserts statistical noise into databases, which makes it challenging to follow data back to particular people. Federated learning greatly lowers the danger of data leaks and unwanted access since it lets models be trained across far-off devices without centralizing data. These technologies offer a necessary first step toward including privacy in the architecture of artificial intelligence systems, even if they are still under development.

Regarding rules, it is absolutely crucial to have strict data security policies. The General Data Protection Regulation (GDPR) of the European Union defines a strong degree of privacy rights. This control covers guidelines for informed permission, data minimization, purpose restriction, and the right to be forgotten. One gets a strong degree of privacy rights. Apart from this, it calls for the responsibility and transparency of data managers and controllers. Although enforcement remains difficult, other areas have either adopted or are working on methods that are similar. Policies should be ready to handle the particular threats presented by artificial intelligence and in line with technical developments. These hazards touch explainability, algorithmic prejudice, and discrimination. Oversight groups, openness tools, and avenues of action help to ensure that privacy rights are not just theoretically enforceable but also practically so.

Changes must be made to the cultural viewpoint and respect society has for personal space. People can undervalue their privacy or see the loss of it as the inevitable result of modern living in a society usually focused on convenience over wisdom. Public education projects, programs teaching digital literacy, and more openness on the side of technology businesses help people to become more educated and empowered. Privacy should be seen as a basic right preserving human dignity, freedom, and democracy rather than as a luxury or a throwback from the past. Furthermore, it is also crucial to challenge the false dichotomy that presents security against privacy. These values are not incompatible; rather, a society that values privacy is more likely to be genuinely secure in a broader sense since it shields people against the arbitrary use of authority. Equally vital are responsibility and openness in monitoring methods. Governments and businesses ought to be open about their data collecting methods, have clear justifications for monitoring operations, and answer for misbehaviour or abuse. Key elements of democratic responsibility are independent inspection agencies, court review, and public reporting. Investigative media and whistleblower protections are also quite important for exposing mistreatment and guiding public opinion. Maintaining the balance between governmental authority and individual rights depends on a watchful civil society enabled to examine and oppose monitoring methods.

The worldwide character of artificial intelligence and data flows, therefore, need international cooperation and standards. Data crosses national boundaries; hence, monitoring policies in one nation can have consequences elsewhere. Common standards and privacy protection in a globalized digital ecosystem need multilateral agreements, worldwide human rights frameworks, and cross-border data security arrangements. Such cooperation has to be based on mutual respect, openness, and the common understanding of privacy as a universal worth.

Finally, one of the most important issues of the digital age is the junction of artificial intelligence, privacy, and monitoring. AI allows hitherto unheard-of levels of surveillance and data exploitation even while it presents strong tools for innovation and societal benefit. In this setting, the protection of privacy is a basic concern about the type of society we want to live in rather than only a technical or legal one. It needs a complete answer, including ethical design, sensible control, public participation informed by knowledge, and worldwide cooperation. We must keep the values of autonomy, dignity, and justice even as we negotiate the promises and hazards of artificial intelligence. Only by doing this will we be able to guarantee that technology advances humanity instead of undercutting the basic pillars of democracy and freedom.

CHAPTER VII

The Future of Artificial Intelligence

AI and Human Collaboration - Discuss how AI can augment, rather than replace, human abilities

It is becoming more and more evident that one of the most transformative events of the modern day is the connection between human cooperation and artificial intelligence. But how artificial intelligence enhances, complements, and expands human talents defines both its present and future path more and more. This is not at all like the bleak picture of machines supplacing people. Artificial intelligence (AI) and human collaboration are the combined interactions between intelligent systems and humans to achieve tasks neither could successfully complete on their own. Among other disciplines, this cooperation covers science, the arts, business, government, and healthcare as well as education. From basic tools to intelligent partners supporting human creativity, decision-making, and problem-solving, artificial intelligence systems are changing their role. As artificial intelligence systems grow increasingly complex, this process is happening. To help design a future in which technology enhances human life in ways that are both significant and ethical, one must first fully grasp the nature of this developing cooperation as well as its possibilities and the difficulties it presents.

First of all, people and artificial intelligence should realize that each of them offers unique benefits of their own. Regarding understanding context, demonstrating empathy, handling uncertainty, and using ethical reasoning, people are really good practitioners. When deciding what to do, people draw on their moral sense, cultural knowledge, and experience. Conversely, artificial intelligence systems are very strong in handling vast volumes of data, identifying trends, completing accurate recurring tasks, and functioning nonstop. These properties combine to create a synergistic relationship whereby artificial intelligence improves human capabilities by raising their speed, scalability, and analytical strength, and human knowledge is directed to guide the algorithms of artificial intelligence. In sectors such as medicine, where artificial intelligence analyses medical imaging or patient data with astonishing speed and accuracy to help doctors detect ailments, this is evident. Stated otherwise, artificial intelligence is enabling physicians to diagnose ailments. Conversely, the doctor is finally in charge of setting the diagnosis in context, interacting with the patient, and suggesting customized treatment depending on a thorough awareness of the patient's general state. This reliance captures the fundamental idea of human-made artificial intelligence cooperation—a mix of human judgment and machine intelligence.

Artificial intelligence is transforming judgments made, team dynamics in the workplace, and job organization as well as other aspects. As knowledge of task-based cooperation grows more advanced, the narrative of automation finally displacing employment is changing. Artificial intelligence is more likely than it is to totally replace tasks in the workplace, especially those that are repetitious or data-intensive, rather than taking over particular roles. This is true because artificial intelligence is more likely to replace jobs needing emotional intelligence, sophisticated thinking, and interpersonal interaction. This, therefore, gives employees an opportunity to focus on activities of higher value, engage in innovative problem-solving, and apply artificial intelligence techniques to raise their output. For example, chatbots are employed in customer service to answer daily routine questions. This releases human agents to concentrate on more complex problems needing empathy and advanced communication. Artificial intelligence can rapidly sort through vast volumes of documents in legal practice to find relevant precedents or evidence. This frees lawyers to focus more on advocacy, negotiation, and strategic needs.

Cooperation between artificial intelligence and humans is also redefining established paradigms in the realm of learning. Using intelligent tutoring systems and adaptive learning platforms to customize their educational experience is becoming more and more common among students. Examining student data helps one to change the curriculum, fill in knowledge gaps, and suggest learning paths. These technologies give teachers insights into the performance and interaction of their pupils, not meant to replace them. Though machines cannot replicate mentoring, inspiration, and emotional support, teachers are able to provide these resources. Particularly in environments when resources are limited or when the needs of the students are varied, this relationship allows one to offer access to more inclusive and efficient education. Furthermore, artificial intelligence offers people customized educational experiences outside of traditional environments, therefore promoting lifetime learning. This will help people to routinely improve their skills in an always changing employment environment.

Scientific research and invention are being enhanced by human and artificial intelligence working together. Artificial intelligence-driven models are used in many different scientific fields, including genetics and climate science, to generate ideas, run experiments, and assess complex information. These abilities enable scientists to focus on completing tasks including result analysis, theory development, and route of future research decision-making. Artificial intelligence models could, in the field of drug discovery, for example, forecast the interactions between chemicals and proteins, therefore drastically saving the time required to find new treatments. Human researchers validate these forecasts by means of clinical experience and experimentation, therefore ensuring that findings are not only morally sound but also practical. This form of cooperation represents a new paradigm of discovery in which artificial intelligence extends the range of human inquiry and accelerates development, not only a question of efficiency.

At this time, artificial intelligence is gradually joining the creative process rather than being limited to analytical tasks in artistic domains, including literature, music, and art. Generative algorithms let one accomplish writing poetry, constructing virtual environments, composing music, and making artwork. One can do the employment of these technologies by artists as co-creators that produce inspiration, investigate alternative ways, or automate regular aspects of the creative process. Still, the human being is still very important in deciding the creative route, evaluating the artistic value of works, and giving them context and significance. While it opens new paths for expression and technological development, the cooperation between artificial intelligence and artists challenges accepted concepts of authorship and creativity. Apart from this, it raises significant philosophical concerns about the nature of creativity and the purpose of aim in artistic projects.

With important implications for quality of life, the healthcare sector offers some of the most remarkable illustrations of human and artificial intelligence cooperating. Artificial intelligence applications are still being used for the aims of diagnosis, patient outcome prediction, treatment approach recommendation, and management of healthcare logistics. While radiologists use artificial intelligence to highly precisely identify abnormalities in imaging scans, doctors use prediction algorithms to construct cancer treatments depending on genetic markers. Artificial intelligence-powered monitoring gadgets used by caretakers and nurses help to track patient circumstances in real time, therefore enabling quick interventions. These tools enhance the capacity of healthcare practitioners to provide fast, accurate, and targeted treatment that is focused on the healthcare recipient; they do not compromise their function as such. The human touch is still indispensable when it comes to comforting patients, guiding moral decisions, and negotiating the challenging emotional dynamics of the healthcare sector.

The ethical and social context of the cooperation between humans and artificial intelligence is among the most important features of it. Successful teamwork requires responsibility, openness, and trust, as well as others. Users must be aware of the functions of artificial intelligence systems, the data on which they depend, and the method of decision-making. This openness helps individuals to make wise decisions regarding when to rely on artificial intelligence and when to ignore its suggestions. It also promotes faith in these systems, which are progressively permeating into vital spheres of daily life. Cooperation suffers in cases when artificial intelligence systems are opaque, surprising, or biased. Making sure artificial intelligence is developed with justice, inclusion, and human involvement will help to build alliances that are both fair and efficient. Furthermore, quite crucial elements in the process of teaching people to operate with artificial intelligence are digital literacy and education. People must be ready with the skills and information required for them to engage meaningfully with intelligent systems, challenge their outputs, and utilize them responsibly.

Human and artificial intelligence work together in the areas of society's governance and decision-making capacities as well. Policymakers use artificial intelligence for the analysis of trends, modelling of policy consequences, and risk assessment in disciplines including public health, urban planning, and environmental management. While human leaders give the values, priorities, and political judgment that machines lack, the employment of these technologies enables one to make judgments more evidence-based and data-driven. To ensure that artificial intelligence-enhanced government will serve the greater interests of society, public participation, and democratic accountability remain important. Simultaneously, ethical frameworks and legal procedures must be developed to supervise artificial intelligence use. This will guarantee that cooperation does not lead to an overindulgence in artificial intelligence, its abuse, or a reduction of human responsibility.

Rather than replacing human labour, the defining feature of the workplace of the future will be the improvement of human potential achieved by means of artificial intelligence. Human and artificial intelligence, used together, will become a major force behind economic growth and creative innovation. The mix of man's strengths and machines is collaborative intelligence. Companies that show a readiness to welcome this synergy will be more suited to adapt to changes, solve challenging issues, and create fresh prospects. This calls for not just technological but also personal investments in individuals. Training, organizational design, and leadership all need to undergo major transformations if we are to build a society of collaboration whereby people and machines may operate in an efficient manner. Human workers and their artificial intelligence counterparts must build trust, interact with one another, and have mutual knowledge of one another if we are to completely enjoy the advantages of this partnership.

The possibility of future cooperation between people and artificial intelligence also motivates reflection on basic traits of human identity, agency, and purpose. With machines today able to complete jobs traditionally assumed to be entirely human, society is being pushed to address issues about what it means to labour, create, and make judgments. Working together with artificial intelligence has the potential to enrich our lives by relieving us of tedious tasks, extending our intellectual and creative horizons, and helping us to solve problems that were once out of our reach, thus reducing the relevance of humans. To fully exploit this promise, though, it is imperative to deliberately ensure that artificial intelligence is developed and used in a way that honours human dignity, autonomy, and well-being. Instead of competing with machines, the aim should be to work with them in the building of a future that reflects our own and the group's objectives and values.

All things considered, the mix of artificial intelligence with human collaboration represents a new horizon in the development of society and technologies. This link is based on complementary strengths, encouragement of one another, and common goals. Artificial intelligence is becoming a more and more powerful friend in many different spheres and disciplines by improving human capacities and creating new paths for invention and expansion. The need for ethical governance, trustworthiness, justice, and openness in the connection makes this cooperation not without challenges. On the other hand, if it is negotiated with great thought, it presents a future in which people and technology will cooperate to create opportunities for flourishing and to solve the most critical issues confronting the world. The degree and nature of our cooperation with intelligent machines will define the world that will arise in the future since artificial intelligence is still under development.

Job Automation and the Future of Work - Consider how AI affects employment and what skills will matter most in an AI-integrated future

The expansion of artificial intelligence and other associated technologies has several consequences, one of which is the possibility of job automation and the future of work. This is among the most important and usually debated of them. Complicated tasks that have traditionally been handled by humans are progressively easier for machines to perform. Civilization is thus at a turning moment of vital intersection. Automation—powered by artificial intelligence, robots, and data-driven decision-making—is changing the way work is done, the types of employment that are accessible, and the very essence of labour. From manufacturing lines to corporate offices, from agricultural to logistics, and even in artistic and professional spheres, the field of intelligent automation is constantly widening. At the same time, this progress is amazing and alarming. It promises to increase efficiency while concurrently cutting prices and liberating people from labour that is either dangerous or monotonous. But it also raises grave issues about rampant unemployment, inequality, and declining job security over time. Not only is it important for governments, businesses, teachers, and employees themselves to grasp how automation changes the job market, but workers also need to know what this suggests about the direction employment will take.

The advent of new technology has always accompanied some degree of disturbance throughout human history. Starting with the steam engine and working on electricity, assembly lines, and personal computers, every new technical development has resulted in the creation of new employment while simultaneously making others obsolete. Many times, these revolutions brought about changes in living standards, higher production, and a restructuring of the economy. Conversely, the degree and pace of automation driven by artificial intelligence are unlike anything else seen previously. Unlike previous technology revolutions, which largely affected physical labour and industrial processes, artificial intelligence is able to automate cognitive tasks, decision-making, and even creative work. This wider reach makes almost every sector vulnerable to change; the shift can happen faster and with more unpredictability than in any other period in history.

The basic premise of automation is that, ultimately, machines would replace human labour for tasks now performed. Its most clear-cut expressions are seen in the industrial sector, where robots are utilized precisely and regularly to complete jobs, including assembly, welding, or warehouse movement of objects. Technologies that either replace or augment human labour in the service company include self-checkout kiosks, customer assistance chatbots, and delivery drones. Offices utilize artificial intelligence systems to do chores, including contract analysis, resume sorting, report generation, and even medical diagnosis support. As natural language processing and computer vision develop, job prospects in fields including journalism, legal research, and picture analysis are becoming more susceptible to automation. Tools driven by artificial intelligence (AI) are enabling customized learning, automation of administrative tasks, and patient care and diagnostics support. This change is happening in fields like education and healthcare, which have long been supposed to be free from the consequences of technological upheaval.

There is no justification for the anxiety about the possible elimination of employment brought about by technology. Many studies aiming at approximating the proportion of employment at risk due to automation have been conducted; their findings have been erratic. Others argue that merely specific functions performed in the workplace will be automated, allowing people to adjust and assume responsibility, complementing their present activities. Some people think that with the existing technology, about half of the jobs that exist could be automated. It is quite clear that the distribution of job automation will not be homogeneous, even if the exact figures are unknown. Particularly those involving predictable and repeated actions, jobs with low degrees of skill and routines are more prone to be risky. Among the jobs in this category are those of cashiers, assembly line workers, and data entry clerks. Concurrent with these improvements in autonomous systems and artificial intelligence, jobs requiring an intermediate degree of knowledge, such as those of administrative assistants or drivers, are in more danger.

Conversely, the application of technology does not always indicate that every employee will be replaced. Most of the time, it changes the fundamental nature of the work instead of totally eradicating it. When some jobs within a field are automated, workers can focus on aspects of their jobs that call for human judgment, sensitivity, or creativity. In the sphere of medicine, for example, artificial intelligence might be utilized to examine X-rays; nonetheless, doctors will still evaluate the data in the framework of the patient's history and render their final decisions. Although artificial intelligence can customize learning resources in the realm of education, instructors will remain indispensable for classroom management and mentoring. Although automated routing software helps the logistics sector to arrange deliveries, human drivers could still be needed to overcome challenging environments or control interactions with clients. The most crucial determinant is people's and companies' capacity to quickly adapt to new roles and processes resulting from automation.

The need for retraining and additional education is among the major challenges automation offers. Others may surface that call for additional skill sets, especially those including digital literacy, problem-solving, teamwork, and adaptability. Should some jobs vanish, other employment that calls for other skill sets will arise. Future professions could need applicants to show ability in communicating with machines, grasping data insights, or running digital platforms. This transition puts governments, training programs, and educational institutions under great pressure to sufficiently equip the workforce for a fast-changing employment market. Throughout one's life, learning should be a need rather than only a goal. Employees should be motivated and given help in their attempts to develop new skills fit for the changing needs of the sector. Public and corporate organizations should engage in education and retraining initiatives if they are to ensure a flawless transition and avoid major numbers of the population from lagging behind.

In addition to the technical skills needed, in this era of automation, the human elements of work are given more importance. Exclusive to humans, abilities including emotional intelligence, creativity, ethical thinking, and interpersonal communication are less likely to be mechanized and hence more sought. The count of occupations requiring caring for other people, understanding complex social issues, or generating creative ideas is expected to rise. Among these are roles in the arts, mental health, education, and the medical sciences. Simultaneous with machines replacing daily tasks, there is a chance that the value of employment linking people, strengthening communities, and enhancing well-being will be increasingly appreciated. Therefore, the future of work might include not only the adaption of technology but also the reassertion of the human purpose of labour and the societal values that it embodies.

The impact of automation on the economy raises still another issue of worry. While automation can help companies save expenses and boost output, it may also create inequality if the advantages of it are not shared fairly. Businesses that effectively apply automation technology could make more profits, but if salaries do not rise proportionately or new employment is not created, money could gather more under the control of capital owners and technological leaders. Workers displaced by technology may find themselves underemployed, unemployed for protracted lengths of time, or downward mobility. This is particularly true in cases when individuals lack choices for social safety nets or retraining programs. One of the possible effects of automation is a polarized labour market whereby a small number of high-skill, high-paying jobs coexist with a great number of low-skill, low-paying ones, hence hollowing out the middle class.

Policymakers' responses to the challenges presented by automation range widely and are always changing. Given the employment uncertainty of today, some advocate universal basic income (UBI) as a means of giving people financial protection. Some people focus especially on making deliberate investments in infrastructure, education, and the employment creation in growing sectors, including green energy, healthcare, and artificial intelligence. Reddening criteria of economic success outside GDP to include indicators of well-being, egalitarianism, and sustainability also attracts increasing interest. These ideas are both growingly significant.

Governments may have to look at fresh approaches to social security, labour laws, and taxes to fit the reality of a workforce always changing. For instance, how should we tax the rise in production brought about by artificial intelligence systems or robots? How may we set up systems to ensure gig workers and freelancers have rights and protections? These questions demand innovative ideas and cooperative solutions involving all pertinent stakeholders—including governments, companies, employees, and members of civil society—that ask for creative ways of thinking.

The future of employment will be determined not only by technology and economics but also by culture and identity. Work has been in charge of giving meaning, direction, and social interaction for a very long period. For many, it provides a sense of success, community, and belonging, as well as the chance to help others. Given the way technology is changing the job scene, it is essential that we also consider the meaning of labour and the possible structures for it that honour human dignity. These covers considering new sorts of jobs, including working from home, with flexible hours, and in cooperative companies. Apart from this, it means fostering cultures in the workplace that give diversity, inclusiveness, and welfare top importance. While technical capacity should be a major determinant of the nature of employment, ethical issues and group objectives should also influence it.

Furthermore, it is important to realize that responsible use of automation has the possibility to be favourable. Less possibly harmful settings for humans can help to lower flaws in important systems and free more time for useful and creative tasks. While reducing their effect on the environment, precision farming could increase agricultural output. Artificial intelligence can assist in early disease identification and treatment regimen improvement in the medical industry. Personalized learning platforms in the realm of education help students to learn at their own speed. These benefits have to be weighed against the possible risks; hence, regulations and procedures emphasizing people's welfare should direct the choice. Guaranteeing that automation will benefit the common good totally depends on the cooperation of engineers, ethicists, legislators, and communities touched by automation.

Furthermore, considered should be the global differences in the consequences of automation. Automation poses a danger to labour-intensive industries, which have historically been the main engines of economic expansion, thereby causing particular problems for emerging nations. Furthermore, possible is their benefit from leapfrogging technologies, which provide for fresh forms of development. To ensure that the benefits of automation are shared equally around the globe and that no country is left behind during this process, international cooperation, information exchange, and fair access to technology will be absolutely crucial.

Ultimately, the nature of employment in this era of automation is not one that one can definitely forecast. The choices we make now shape our present as well as our future: how we build technology, prioritize values, and develop economies. Though automation presents major challenges, it also presents a once-in-a-lifetime chance to rethink and reinterpret the purpose of work in the framework of society. By means of human-centred development, inclusive growth, and lifelong learning, we may build a future whereby employment remains a source of both inspiration and goal-oriented activity. Regarding automation, the goal should be to maximize its possibilities rather than to oppose it so that everyone may live in a more equitable, fair, and happy environment. Our decisions now at this pivotal junction will decide whether or not automation worsens divisions or whether it creates the path for a new era of shared riches and human flourishing.

CONCLUSION

As shown by examples relevant to the real world and easily understandable, artificial intelligence (AI) is more than just a technological trend; it is a defining force of the twenty-first century. From tailored recommendations to cutting-edge medical diagnostics, artificial intelligence is silently driving developments almost across every sphere of our lives. Our lives are fast being transformed by these inventions. Comprehending the principles of its operation is no longer a specialized ability; rather, it is a basic component of digital literacy.

Over the whole book, "Artificial Intelligence Fundamentals: Understanding Modern Machine Learning Concepts - Discover AI Basics Through Approachable, Real-World Examples," we have looked at the basic ideas behind artificial intelligence and machine learning in an approachable and grounded on particular instances from daily life manner. You now know the several forms of learning, how algorithms make decisions, and how artificial intelligence finds use in language, vision, prediction, and other fields. You also know the challenges artificial intelligence (AI) presents, which range from ethical quandaries to data bias, as well as the need to create AI systems that are responsible and centred on people.

Inspired to delve further into technical learning, investigate ethical issues, or just feel more confident interacting with artificial intelligence in your daily life, this book has given you a strong basis. Both of these are plausible. Equipped with your newly acquired knowledge, you are ready to participate in the still-underwritten future of artificial intelligence.

Thank you for buying and reading/ listening to our book. If you found this book useful/ helpful please take a few minutes and leave a review on the platform where you purchased our book. Your feedback matters greatly to us.

www.ingramcontent.com/pod-product-compliance
Lightning Source LLC
LaVergne TN
LVHW022057200926
848481LV00003B/954
9798349303531